PRAISE FOR
WAITING FOR OUR SOULS
TO CATCH UP
By Carol M. Perry, SU

"Of the hundreds of books we have read in 2014, this slim little volume by a Roman Catholic nun has affected us most. Written with warmth and wit, *Waiting for Our Souls to Catch Up* offers specific, simple ways to help people find God in everyday life. A delight for the believer or the seeker on your list."

— *Deirdre Donahue and Christina Ianzito*
"The Best Books of 2014," AARP

D1210480

Also By Carol M. Perry, SU

Waiting for Our Souls to Catch Up

*Called and Sent: A Brief History of the
Society of Saint Ursula*
(with Agnes McManus, SU)

AMONG WOMEN

LIVES OF CHALLENGE, COURAGE AND FAITH IN BIBLICAL TIMES

~ ~ ~ ~ ~

CAROL M. PERRY, SU

/-/ /

Asahina & Wallace
Los Angeles
2016

Published in the United States by Asahina & Wallace, Inc.
(www.asahinaandwallace.com)

ISBN: 978-1-940412-18-4
Library of Congress Control Number: 2016931057

Contents

PREFACE

The Bible never ceases to amaze me. I once rather inelegantly compared reading it to peeling an onion. One can carefully remove layer after layer and there is always a new one. This has been my experience with the Bible. One verse of a text highlights another one that I don't remember seeing before, and I find myself going down a new road to a new adventure.

That is what has led me to write this book. It is not a work of biblical scholarship. The past forty years have given us many thoughtful and provocative pieces of research from scholars intent on analyzing biblical texts on women. I can add nothing there.

This is not a book of devotional reading on biblical women. There is a small library of those books from some of our best spiritual writers. I would not add anything there.

Rather, this is a human look at some of the named and nameless women to be found in the heritage that is the Bible. Having spent more than half my life teaching the Bible in interdenominational settings, I bring to these reflections my love of the riches of biblical study across standard religious borders.

Some readers might be led by the title to

make links to the words of a Catholic prayer in honor of Mary. (In chapter 8 you will find the words in their original context.) These reflections are really an invitation to step into the Bible from wherever you are and to consider these women just as they are. They belong to no denomination, since they come from the pages of a text that is open to each of us, male or female, of any religious background whatsoever or of no particular religious tradition.

The situations in which these women find themselves are not prescriptive for us, but rather allow us to see ourselves in their very human experiences. As we ponder what they did — and ask what we might have done — so much becomes clearer for our own journeys.

We see here the powerful and the powerless, the married and the widowed, the saintly and the sinner. They span almost two thousand years of history and they live in worlds that are not ours. Neither their living situations nor the customs that hem them in are familiar. All that they have in common with each other and with us is that they are women. That is how they confront us.

As we do, they make decisions and then live with the results. Some of them are rebels. Some of them are lawbreakers. Some find a way to newness through the coils of legalities and customs. Some change history and some are changed by it. Some are conformists and some are searchers for a new route. None is boring.

It is with that in mind that I invite you to look at them. You might be inspired or fired up with fury at what they face, or drawn to smile as they circumvent those in power, but you will not find them dull.

They are my friends, women I have come to know through my own study and teaching. I want you to meet them too and to ask yourself what you might have done had you been in their circumstances.

There is your challenge.

Introduction

Meet my friends. They could be your neighbors, cousins, sisters, mothers. They aren't. Because of history and culture, time and geography, they live in another world, but they share our human condition.

They too love, agonize, decide. Sometimes their circumstances demand that they say "yes" and move blindly forward into the always unknowable future. Sometimes the only reply is "no." That might be quiet defiance or an audible stand against injustice. Sometimes there is support from another; at other times, they stand alone, trembling but resolved.

In some circumstances they move tentatively, as we often do, not quite sure about what they are involved in, but most trust God to help them find a way. However, we will also meet those who plot evil. The biblical world is real, with room for the good and the bad. Human nature is on full display here!

In these pages we will meet certain women for the first or maybe the twenty-first time. Many of their names are known. Others might be unfamiliar. Still others speak from the pages of the Bible with no identity other than that which their society gave them: wife, mother, or simply "a woman." We so often want to know more but their record is sparse.

Although their circumstances are not ours, the real woman within is recognizable.

I never cease to be amazed to find "real" women in the Bible, living certainly in a very different world, but women of courage and ingenuity and with a keen sense of humor. Yes, they are all in the Bible!

I would like you to meet some of them too. Where scholarship helps, I will not hesitate to refer to it, but what I really hope will happen is that you might come to see these wives and sisters, mothers and daughters, as friends, people with whom you could break bread or share coffee. If they become that real then they will find their way into your reflective life without my making any overt effort to help you.

What the Bible does is describe the world these women inhabited. It has no choice. However, because it is a society that is not ours we can neither simply ignore it nor should we think it necessary to adopt it. This is why the way we read the Bible is so important. The human authors are telling us that this is how things were, not how they should be for every time and place.

Just as we read history and do not fault Martin Luther for not having sent a text message about his theological issues nor blame George Washington for not phoning ahead before crossing the Delaware, we have no right to blame any biblical woman for not doing what we might have done with our cultural background. She lived in another world, a world I will attempt to describe as we meet each of these women.

Because a book of the Bible tells us how these people lived, it is not saying that this is how we are to live. We have also to remind ourselves that the Bible is a library spanning centuries. A nomadic Sarah in a polygamous society shapes her life by factors that are so different from those of urban Priscilla eighteen hundred years later. Each deals with her circumstances, as must we.

This point is so important because critics are inclined to make this incredible library a weapon of patriarchy. How society was shaped then is not how society should be shaped today. In every age women and men have to make their way in the world in which they live. This is the intriguing fact about the women we will meet during our study. Each one says, "I chose to do this. You might or might not have made the same choice, but see me for who I am and when I lived."

Much of the Bible is patriarchal and we owe it to the pursuit of truth to try to understand its broad strokes. It is hard for us to think of a world where a woman was always in the care of a man. This was for her protection in a largely agricultural world where the family line depended upon new life and where few women could work outside the home.

That home was the unit that provided food, clothing, medical care, "retirement benefits," and safety to every inhabitant across generational lines. The more people available in one's family, the richer one was.

In a household unit, a girl was taught the skills she would need by her mother, grandmother, and possibly sisters-in-law, the wives of her elder brothers. Her father, or if he were dead, the eldest male family member, had the responsibility of finding a suitable spouse for her. Love grew afterwards in the life shared, although we will meet a striking couple whose love preceded their being wed.

Since a girl's marrying meant that she was impoverishing her birth household and adding to the wealth of her husband's, gifts had to be given by the new family to make up for her loss. That is how the dowry originated.

There are two reasons why the cultures of the Near Eastern world so valued sons. They would bring another woman into the household, where she would be welcomed and where the male was seen to be the life-giver. A little biblical biology can help here. For the entire Old and New Testaments and on into the Middle Ages, male sperm was considered to be the source of life. The woman merely received his "offering" and she became a kind of walking incubator. She made no other biological contribution. Hence, if life did not follow a sexual union, it had to be her fault, and she was labeled "barren." I will pass no judgment on these ancestors since we were almost in modern times before the biology of sexual intercourse was accurately understood.

Life expectancy was short in these early days. The average biblical male was dead in his forties, having survived his childbearing wife by about ten years. It would also be a long time before a concept of life after death is held, so this life was all. A man could only live on in his sons, who would be named, for example, Jacob, son of Isaac. Hence, every time this Jacob was mentioned, his father's name was kept alive. (This accounts for the lengthy identification of males in the Bible.)

A woman, if she is named, is identified as "wife of" or "daughter of." Thought to have had no part in the creation of her children, she is rarely named with them, except for the kings of Israel. Their mothers are often named, chiefly because of the honor involved.

Polygamy thus almost naturally became the norm across the entire biblical world during this agricultural era. The more women, the more hands to do the household work and the more wombs to bear children. (Polyandry, that is, a woman with multiple male partners, was not practiced because there would be no way to determine paternity.) Gradually, as the world became more urbanized, polygamy would die out. By the time of the New Testament, it has almost vanished.

The household unit, to which a young man brought his bride, with the newly built addition to his father's property, still persisted in the first century of our era. Jesus almost certainly grew up in some kind of extended family: cousins, uncles, aunts, possibly grandparents in a family house or compound. We in the Western world have to remind ourselves that this kind of family was the norm in much of America into the twentieth century. The modern nuclear family would have been viewed, biblically, as poor, lacking the "wealth" of many hands and hearts.

We have to grasp this very basic idea of family if the biblical stories are to make sense. To this day, across most of Africa and Asia, similar family units are still the norm. Within them our biblical woman would still feel at home.

In the pages that follow, we are going to meet some of these women, grouped by their reactions to the circumstances in which they find themselves. They make decisions, and we are going to become part of them. Let us begin.

~1~

WOMEN WHO SAID "NO"

THE EXODUS WOMEN; THE DAUGHTERS OF ZELOPHEHAD; ABIGAIL; THE WOMAN WITH THE FLOW OF BLOOD

Sometimes circumstances are such that the only response to a situation is a resounding "no." Let's meet some of these biblical naysayers and see what happened because of their refusals to go along with circumstances or customs.

~THE EXODUS WOMEN~

While we all know something of the Moses story, we do not often reflect on the fact that it took five strong women to bring him into life and to ready him for God's work, beginning with his birth mother, Jochebed, who could not bear to obey the Pharaoh and see Moses die at birth. She is abetted by two extraordinary midwives, Shiphrah and Puah, whose lively dialogue with the Pharaoh is worth studying. (Exodus 1-2)

This unnamed Egyptian ruler has become upset by the continued proliferation of the Hebrew people who occupy land near the border. He imagines their possibly joining an invader to overwhelm Egypt. He is also a man who does not know the history of his country and that one of these Hebrews, Joseph, saved the land from famine years before. He blindly issues an order to the midwives of Egypt that all Hebrew males are to be killed at birth. That will end the population growth among the Hebrews. When it becomes obvious that his order is being ignored, he sends for the Hebrew midwives to find out why.

The humor in their answer totally escapes him but it is clear to the biblical reader. They tell him that the Hebrew women are not like the Egyptians. They give birth before the midwives arrive. "We are too late," they lament. The puzzled monarch actually believes that the Hebrews are a race different from the Egyptians. Not only does he swallow their story, but they escape his punitive wrath.

Meanwhile, little Moses is nursed at home as long as possible and when he can no longer be hidden, he is placed in a basket among the bulrushes, guarded by his watchful older sister who waits to see what might happen should he be spotted by a passerby.

Against all odds, it is a daughter of the Pharaoh himself who sees the child and who adopts him as her own, thus assuring him an Egyptian education and a future. She even pays his own mother to nurse him until he is ready for palace food.

While young Moses grows up in the Pharaoh's palace, he sees his own people cruelly enslaved as the Egyptians try to destroy the Hebrews. The latter are brickmakers and bricklayers for the ongoing building projects of Egypt. We are not told how Moses knows where he belongs by birth, but he obviously is aware of the suffering of his people, which he has escaped through the actions of his mother, the midwives, his sister, and the Pharaoh's daughter.

These five women connive, against all odds, to give the future leader life and health, each one defying the law in her own way. Interestingly, only the midwives are named at this point in the narrative, a sure sign that their part in the story was known and loved. We can only wonder if, years later when Moses appears before the Pharaoh to ask for the liberation of his people, it is this "grandfather Pharaoh" who sits on the throne.

Did this ruler have any idea what his daughter had done? Was her place in the palace so separate that an adopted Hebrew child could grow to adulthood unknown to the ruler? The possibilities are interesting to ponder even as we reflect on the cumulative power of five women defiant in the face of injustice.

~THE DAUGHTERS OF ZELOPHEHAD~

Our next encounter is with women in a different situation that calls for action. Much time has passed and an adult Moses has led the Israelites out of Egypt and across a desert where they have been formed into a people ready for the next phase of their lives in the Promised Land. (Numbers 27; 36)

The desert living is almost over and the survivors are being allotted land grants in the territory they are about to occupy. It is an all-male roll call until Moses comes to the family of Zelophehad. The patriarch of this family was a good man who had died in the desert, leaving as his survivors five daughters, but no sons. By law, there is no one eligible to receive land. These feisty girls will not have it so. At some point they put their collective heads together and say that there is no reason for them to be overlooked. The uncle responsible for their marriages is going to have a hard time placing five landless and penniless girls in good households. The girls make a decision.

They come to Moses and plead their case. To his everlasting credit, he does not dismiss their request. Does he remember those women who were so crucial to his own survival? All the Bible tells us is that he brought their case "before the Lord." This offers the possibility of imagining what might have passed between them: Moses, unsure of the conse-

19

quences of allowing women to have land, consults a God who seems willing to move with Israel in a new direction. Moses emerges from the Meeting Tent to announce a change in Israelite law: "If a man dies and has no son, then you shall pass his inheritance on to his daughter."

Those five girls are all named for us as Mahlah, Noah, Hoglah, Milcah, and Tirzah. This in itself is a rarity. What is more amazing is their refusal to accept an unjust status quo. One has to wonder what transpired around the campfires that evening as the Hebrew women nudged each other with glee and the men must have wondered: "What might happen next?"

It didn't take long for some of the diehard legalists to point out the defect in this new law. If the girls should marry outside their tribe and take their inheritance with them, some other tribe would have a land increase. Not a good idea!

So an adjustment is made to the rule of female inheritance. In the case of extra-tribal marriage, the land cannot be transferred. (Numbers 36) In actuality, the daughters of Zelophehad are not affected by this amendment since they marry within the clan. They must have been much sought-after brides, bringing an unusual dowry to their suitors, since they are the first landed women we meet. What is more astonishing is that their resistance to what they perceive as an injustice leads to a change in universal law.

~ABIGAIL~

Our next naysayer springs full-bodied from 1 Samuel 25. Several hundred years have passed and Israel as a nation is settled in the valley and on the hills of the Promised Land. There is a kind of civil war roiling the land. Saul has been chosen as the first king but has proven unworthy of the throne. David has been anointed to succeed him, but has to wait until Saul dies to take his place as ruler. So David roams the Sinai area with a band of hired mercenaries. One season finds him in the open grazing lands of the Sinai Peninsula in the territory of a certain Nabal. The text is blunt in describing Nabal: "The man was surly and mean; he was a Calebite."

That doesn't quite say it all since the drama heightens when the Bible adds that Nabal is married to a woman named Abigail who we are told is both clever and beautiful. We are soon to learn just how clever she is.

Throughout the long grazing season David has restrained his men, not allowing them to poach from the various herders who are using the broad fields to fatten their animals. It is an understood but unwritten law that if such wanderers respect the flocks of an owner and even perhaps supply a bit of protection they could claim the right of a reward in the form of an animal when sheepshearing takes place.

Shearing season is a relaxed, celebratory, festive time, marked by hard work and plenty of food, a huge barbecue being part of it. Owners feel generous, having successfully made it through the long grazing time with flocks still intact.

David makes his move by sending some of his young men to Nabal with a reminder that he has respected Nabal's flock. They request the usual token of thanks. Nabal lives up to his name, "fool," with a most ungracious reply: "Who is David? Who is the son of Jesse? … Shall I take my bread and my water and the meat that I have butchered for my shearers and give it to men who come from I do not know where?"

Stung by the rejection, David's men return to him and he acts as anyone would who saw that his respect and restraint were being ignored. David thunders: "Every man strap on his sword!" It is a battle cry as the fully armed group heads up the mountain passes to exact their revenge.

But there are cooler heads at Nabal's ranch. One of his workmen has sought out Abigail to tell her what has transpired. He emphasizes the honesty of David's group, which had been providing protection during the long weeks of grazing.

This servant also must know something of the character of the mistress of the household because he says: "Now therefore know this and consider what you must do." Has she before had to undo some of the evil work of her surly spouse?

Abigail is as quick thinking as she is lovely. She knows that the household will be slaughtered because of her husband's actions. She literally raids the pantry, packing loaves of bread, skins of wine, measures of grain, and clusters of raisins and figs onto the backs of donkeys. There is little time to lose.

In a scene worthy of being filmed, she starts down the mountainside as David, muttering threats of total annihilation, is coming up. She blocks the narrow defile, slides from her animal to the ground and begins a long speech of apology. "Nabal is his name, and folly is with him." Thus punning on the meaning of Nabal, she pleads for restraint.

She does not pause long enough to allow David to speak. She is literally talking for her life. Abigail wisely reminds David that he is destined to rule and he should not come to power with blood on his hands. She pleads for him to remember the Lord his God, which makes us wonder about Abigail's own background. She is seemingly not of Israel but she knows that David worships a God who is involved in his life.

David is totally disarmed by her reasoning, her beauty, and her generosity as he sees the laden animals just waiting to feed his men. There is no need to kill for more. He sends her home in peace.

Abigail returns to the celebratory sheep-shearers at her husband's tables, but is unable to speak to Nabal. It is a masculine party and we are told that Nabal is very drunk. His wife waits until morning and, "when the wine had gone out of him," he learns that he has escaped death and the destruction of his household through the cleverness of Abigail. He could not have been pleased. After all, it was his household and it was his goods that she has distributed. "His heart died within him; he became like a stone." Stroke? Heart attack? Whatever it was, in ten days he is dead.

David is not ungrateful. He does for Abigail what the culture of the day would have expected. He woos her and she accepts him, becoming his third wife. While she is listed in the family line with her son, it seems as if that child must not have survived to adulthood, and neither of them is heard from again.

However, Abigail remains as a vivid portrait of a woman who will not allow her entire household to be massacred because of the limited vision of a foolish husband. It is remarkable that her story comes to us from the patriarchal world in which she lived.

~THE WOMAN WITH THE FLOW OF BLOOD~

One can say no to rulers, to husbands, to the laws of society, but it is so much harder to stand against the unwritten prejudices of an entire society. We have to go to the Gospels to find an unnamed woman who is so daring. (Mark 5: 25–34)

In a clearly drawn vignette, Jesus has just returned to Capernaum from the other side of the Sea of Galilee. He is immediately entreated by Jairus, head of the synagogue, to come and lay his hand upon his young daughter who is dying. Surrounded by crowds, pushing and jostling, Jesus is making his way down the street when he suddenly halts and says, "Who touched me?"

It isn't hard to imagine the faces of his disciples. They are incredulous. Who didn't touch him in that crowd? Jesus stands still and waits. A trembling woman comes forward and kneels before him.

Her story is pitiful. She has been ill, suffering from a flow of blood for twelve years. In a world that equated blood with life, she is seen as a kind of walking dead person. She is not allowed to be part of the village scene lest she contaminate others. Most probably she has been dependent upon the kindness of the village women to go to the market for her. There has been no place for her at the village well, source of water and female friendship, no possibility of her using the village oven. She is seen by all as unclean. No physician can help her. She has tried them all. She has no hope.

This day she has seized control of her life. She will not be a victim any longer. If the doctors are useless, there is still one hope. His name is Jesus. So, she has defied the rule that says she cannot mingle with others. She has thrust herself into the crowd with this decision. "I don't need to speak to him. All I need to do is to touch the edge of his cloak." This is the faith that motivates her.

Jesus knows this. He stands stock-still and looks around at all those faces while an impatient Jairus taps his foot. Jesus has time. She comes forward fearfully to tell her story and Jesus listens. Then he says the words that restore her to life.

"Daughter, your faith has made you well. Go in peace." Daughter: She is an outsider no longer but is part of the family. To her healed body Jesus gives the further balm of a new sense of self.

Before that day is over, Jesus will give back to Jairus his daughter, a child whose age matches all the years this other member of the human family had suffered her shame and social rejection. That evening in Capernaum there must have been a celebration at the home of the synagogue leader. He is a loving father who has brought Jesus to his dying child. There must also have been a secondary festive meal for the friends of this woman of faith, nameless but not faceless. Her family has suddenly grown so large since Jesus has claimed her. Her terrors as she planned her move are almost forgotten as she stands in the doorway of her home, erect and well, ready to reclaim life.

Her defiance, born of desperation, has given her a new life. She might be anonymous but she stands beside her predecessors who knew when and how to say "no." They are an assortment, aren't they? Midwives to an enslaved people, an unnamed Egyptian princess, five girls who suffer from the crime of being women in a world that overlooked them, a wise wife who cannot permit her husband's selfishness to lead to the death of an entire household, and a village woman who has simply had enough.

None of them knows if her defiance will mean life or death. Each of them knows that the status quo can stand no longer. There is much to ponder here.

~2~

WOMEN WHO SAID "YES"

REBEKAH; RAHAB; HULDAH; THE DAUGHTERS OF SHALLUM; MARY OF NAZARETH; THE BENT-OVER WOMAN

Sometimes life demands a vigorous "yes" to a circumstance. There are biblical women who discover that this is their vocation. One of the most vividly portrayed of these is found in the patriarchal stories of Genesis 24.

~REBEKAH~

Abraham is growing old and has real concerns about the marriage of his son Isaac. Living as a wandering herdsman, Abraham has no access to his family roots and he cannot bear to think of Isaac bringing a stranger into the familial tent. So he calls his eldest servant and charges him to go back to the land he had left and to seek a wife for Isaac there. It is a solemn charge and the servant accepts it, loads ten of his master's camels, and sets out for the mountains to the north.

On the road, he shrewdly plots his course of action as he prays to the God of his master. Obviously, the God of Abraham is not his deity but he addresses the One who he thinks will bring about the desired outcome. This servant is a practical man who knows the kind of strength the right wife might need. So he asks that when he reaches his destination and takes his place at the town well, the girl of destiny will not only accede to his request for a drink but will offer to water the camels as well. This will be no small task after a long journey!

His prayer is barely ended before Rebekah, grandniece of Abraham, comes with her water jar on her shoulder. The girl is "very fair to look upon." She passes the visual test. The servant moves forward and asks for a sip of water. She agrees as she adds, "I will draw water for your camels also." Indeed here is an answer to prayer.

As Rebekah completes her tasks, the servant draws forth from his bag "a gold nose ring weighing half a shekel, and two bracelets for her arms weighing ten gold shekels." In a world without hotels, she makes the next move and invites him to stay with her family. She dashes on ahead to announce his arrival and to show the proof of his wealth. Her brother Laban, the head of the household, comes out to endorse the invitation. The camels are stabled, the familial ties are established, and a meal is prepared.

However, the ever-diligent servant refuses to eat until he has explained the reason for his journey, to find a wife for his master's son. Rebekah fits the bill. Her brother agrees, with words that sound harsh to modern ears: "Look, Rebekah is before you, take her and go, and let her be the wife of your master's son, as the Lord has spoken." (Genesis 24: 51)

But this young woman is no parcel to be wrapped and sent on its way. She is a clearly drawn personality and she has obviously been cheering from the sidelines for this happy change in her life. Why had no eligible man sought her hand until now? Was she too innovative? Or is it possible that this family too was living among strangers and her brother hesitated to marry her into a foreign tribe?

We will never know but, after the customary exchange of gifts, the men celebrate with a festive meal. Did the women have their own party in the kitchen, a time to examine the rings and bracelets and other gifts? As the food is shared so too are speculations about the future.

The next morning, the servant is ready to go home. His task has been accomplished and he wants to get back to Abraham with the good news. Rebekah's family asks for a ten-day delay, presumably to make adequate preparations. The servant demurs. Abraham cannot wait. At this impasse, something unusual happens. The men of the family say, "We will call the girl and ask her."

They do. Is she ready, with less than a day's notice, to mount a camel and travel several hundred miles to marry a man whose name, Isaac, means laughter? It is an entirely unknown world out there and there will be no turning back.

Her answer is clear and enthusiastic. To their "Will you go with this man?" she joyously replies, "I will."

And so, blessed by those she is leaving, and most probably wearing her new jewelry, Rebekah rides out of town and down the road to her future. In a lovely turn in the storytelling of Genesis, we are given a glimpse of Isaac in verse 63, walking in the fields as evening falls. He must have been understandably anxious about the outcome of a journey in which he had no voice.

As Isaac looks up, he sees camels on the horizon. Rebekah spots him at the same moment and modestly adjusts her veil. In memorable words, Genesis says, "He took Rebekah and she became his wife, and he loved her."

Her immediate "yes" to the unknown rings out clearly to the Bible reader. This spirited young woman brings a sense of excitement into the patriarchal story where her twin sons, Esau and Jacob, will have a lasting place in history.

~RAHAB~

We find another adventuresome woman in the book of Joshua, chapter 2. The Israelites are poised to enter the Promised Land. Moses has died and been buried, and the man who was his assistant all through the desert years has assumed the leadership role. Joshua is well trained and has learned, from his own experience, the value of scouts. So he sends two young men across the Jordan River to spy on the land, especially the city of Jericho, which stands before them.

They go and find their way into the house of a prostitute, Rahab. Had her reputation penetrated even the desert? We are left to wonder how the spies knew of her, but it proves to be a fortuitous choice. This Rahab is astute in the ways of the world. She knows that the king of Jericho will be informed almost immediately so she hides the men, cleverly taking them to the roof of her house and hiding them among the stalks of flax that are drying there. When the knock sounds on her door, she can truthfully say to the king's henchmen that the men are no longer in her house. (The Bible loves such plays on words!)

With a straight face, Rahab urges pursuit of the foreigners, even suggesting that they had better hurry if they would overtake the spies. They obediently take off across the plain.

Meanwhile, Rahab returns to the roof to bargain for her reward. She says that she knows the Lord is on the side of Israel and that it is only a matter of time before Jericho will be in their hands. She asks that, as she has risked her life for the spies, they in turn remember to deal kindly with her and her family on the day of the invasion. Since Rahab mentions her father and mother, brothers and sisters, it seems as if she is the support of the entire group, quite a reversal of the usual familial structure.

The Israelite spies agree, requesting that on the day of the great battle she should gather the family into her house, tie a crimson cord at the window, and stay put until the invasion is over.

Rahab urges the spies to head for the hill country to the west for three days. Then, when the pursuit has ended, they can safely cross the Jordan and rejoin Joshua. The agreement is struck and in a cinematic moment, she lets the spies down through her window, which must have been part of the walls of Jericho. They safely follow through on her flight plan.

The eventual fall of Jericho remains a bit of a mystery even to archeologists — timely earthquake? Surrender of the city because of psychological warfare? All the records show is that Jericho falls and the family of Rahab is rescued. (Joshua 6:25) Her trust is rewarded.

We are left with much about which to muse. How did this pagan woman know of Israel? What motivated her to feel such responsibility for her family? How did the spies land on her doorstep?

Rahab finds herself in a situation, seizes on the best solution to her problem, and is faithful to her word. The Israelites are true to theirs as well. It is an early indication of the power of the spoken word to bind those concerned. A woman of somewhat questionable morality is the gateway into the Promised Land.

~HULDAH~

Centuries elapse between Rahab and the next woman of the hour, Huldah. (2 Kings 22:13–20) We find ourselves somewhere near the end of the seventh century BC and Israel is in danger of losing the Land of Promise. The armies of Babylon are on the move against Jerusalem. Faithless kings and a religiously indifferent people have stirred the prophets to anger and to pleas to repent before it is too late. Their messages have fallen on deaf ears. A religiously smug city has taken refuge in the belief that God would never let anything happen to his city. Since the word of God rests in the Ark of the Covenant within the Temple, Jerusalem will always be protected from harm.

At this moment a young king, Josiah, comes to power. He wants to restore Jerusalem to its earlier glory so he begins by renovating the Temple, which has fallen into disuse and neglect. A veritable army of carpenters and masons is hired for the task. One day they make a great discovery. In a dusty storage space they find the book of the Law and bring it to the king. It seems to be part of Leviticus, a moldering scroll that lists the festivals of Israel, none of which is being observed. What is to be done?

A prophet must be consulted for advice, but to whom should the king go? At this time, there are two major male prophets in Jerusalem: Jeremiah, who is being shaped by God for his future work, and Ezekiel, who is his contemporary and who must have been active as well. They cannot be unknown to Josiah. He ignores them and sends his carefully selected delegates to Huldah, a named woman prophet.

She is introduced as married to Shallum, keeper of the wardrobe. His parentage is listed, supposedly giving her status, and their address, the Second Quarter of Jerusalem, is also to be found. These odd bits of identity, plus her name, make Huldah stand out on the pages of her story. What no one notes is the trepidation she must have felt when the ad hoc committee, led by the priest Hilkiah, arrives on her doorstep to ask her to consult

the Lord for the king. Is it a trap? Has she
been chosen so that, if the message is dire, it
might be ignored as coming from a woman?
To say yes or no could be equally dangerous.

Huldah is true to the mission she has received from God. Asked to consult for the
king, she does just that and bluntly offers
God's answer. It is not encouraging. Idolatry
has provoked the wrath of God and Jerusalem is destined for destruction. Her hearers'
faces must have blanched at this. However,
all the news is not bleak. Because the king has
tried to do what is right, disaster will not
happen in his lifetime. His eyes will be closed
in death before the city falls.

Josiah humbly listens to the report and
then proceeds to act. He gathers together the
elders of Israel and institutes religious reform.
There is enormous courage in this action of a
young king who could have said, "What's the
use?" He feels it his duty to try. Stirred by the
words of Huldah he does just that.

In imitation of the leaders of old he re-
news the covenant, reading from the tattered
and forgotten book that had been unearthed
by the temple workmen. The text of our Bible, as so often happens, does not tell us all
we would like to know. Is Huldah in that
crowd of people pledging to be faithful? If
she is, we can be sure she keeps her promise,
even as the others gradually push aside all

thoughts of religious reform and slide back into their old ways.

Huldah's task is to speak the word. With courage, she does just that and we are left to ruminate on this fearless woman. She has not been expunged from the record. Does she live long enough to know that the valiant young king dies in battle? Does she witness the futility of his successors? Does she live to see her city of dreams invaded by Babylon? As this enemy destroys the Temple do the clouds of dust drift over to her residence in the Second Quarter? There are so many questions and so few answers from a woman standing at the crossroads of history.

~THE DAUGHTERS OF SHALLUM~

We do not know the fate of Huldah but we do know the fate of so many others who are led by the conquering Babylonians out of ruined Jerusalem and sent on the long march to the city of Babylon. This kind of forced exile or repopulation was so common in the ancient world. Once in Babylon, the exiles are not imprisoned. They are free to find work or to starve. Their survival depends on themselves. The only thing they cannot do is to go home.

Ezekiel has come with them and these four decades prove to be a fertile time of religious renewal. Gradually, they begin to see that their God is not a God of the Land of Promise, but a God of the Word. No matter where they go and no matter what happens to their place of worship, God is present in his word to them. Most scholars believe that this is a time when the Bible begins to be put together in written form, when the psalms they have been singing in many parts of the land are collected into one book, and when the ancestor stories are given their final written form after centuries of oral existence.

It is also inevitable that Jerusalem comes to mean different things to different segments of the population. The old long to go home and once again enter the courts of the Lord. Some of the new generation that have never seen Temple or city are eager for the freedom to travel and to carry God's word with them wherever they go. Others have absorbed the dreams of parents or grandparents and want to return. Meanwhile, on the banks of the rivers that run through Babylon, the Jews, as they are now called, begin to develop a rudimentary synagogue service. They have no building, but they have their songs of praise and petition, and they can retell the actions of God in the lives of those who have gone before them. They wait.

The time of their deliverance does come when a new force in history, Persia, rises up to conquer Babylon. Cyrus, the Persian king, grants the right to return to all the captive people he has inherited. He asks that they rebuild their altars and he furnishes funds for this to happen. He gives safe conduct to all returnees from any nation. All he asks in return is that these people pray for him.

Cyrus generates enormous goodwill by his benevolence, frees his armies from the task of supervising disgruntled exiles, and prepares for a new future of conquering the world. It is not surprising that the book of Isaiah speaks of him in glowing terms as a true gift from God. The Babylonian Exile is over.

The long journey back to Jerusalem begins, some five hundred miles along the edge of the Fertile Crescent to a city that many of them have never seen. The returnees are a motley group, some of the very old living in their dreams of what was, some of the very young seeking adventure; the religiously fervent rubbing elbows with the politically hopeful who long to be anyplace except in Babylon. It is not hard to fill in the blanks. What they find is discouraging.

The walls of the city are a tumble of rocks. The houses they remember, if they are still standing, are occupied by others who have moved in over the long decades. The gardens of grandfather are only overgrown weeds and the vineyards have not been cultivated. Their traditional enemies from Samaria have been making inroads. Is it any wonder that the first weeks are a time of more grief and futility? The messages that go back to relatives in Babylon are discouraging.

Among these is a young Jew named Nehemiah, serving as cupbearer to the king and avidly reading the news that reaches him from Jerusalem. He finally asks the king for permission for a leave of absence so that he might go to Jerusalem and help his people rebuild. In the ancient world if a city has no gates and walls, it is not really a city. Nehemiah longs to set things in motion since a pall of discouragement has fallen on the pioneers.

A most obliging ruler gives his consent and Nehemiah sets out. (Nehemiah 2) He reaches a ruined city that indeed has no walls. Ever practical, Nehemiah makes a circuit of Jerusalem to assess the situation, riding his animal as far as he can, making note of the burned gates and piles of stone. In a scene not hard to imagine, he saddles his donkey and rides around the destroyed city by moonlight. He wants none of the enemies to see him. When even his sure-footed beast can go no further, Nehemiah makes his way on foot, marking what needs to be done. Then he gathers together the leaders of the people and firmly announces: "Come, let us rebuild the wall of Jerusalem." His positive energy fills the dispirited among the returnees, and they enthusiastically join him.

But Nehemiah is not just a dreamer. He has a plan. Looked at whole, the task is enormous. Divided into bite-sized pieces, it is doable, so he challenges the Jews to each be responsible for a section of the wall. Nehemiah 3 is one of the more remarkable records in the Bible. It lists every person working on the wall, who he was and exactly what he was about. Note is duly made of the shirkers: "...but their nobles would not put their shoulders to the work of their Lord." (Nehemiah 3:5)

This litany of laborers is meticulous in assuring that no one is omitted and that posterity will know that the rich carried stones beside the poor, that gatekeepers and merchants, Levites and priests, goldsmiths and perfume makers all played their part.

To be noted is verse 12, which records that Shallum, "leader of half the district of Jerusalem," thus a local politician of some sort, made repairs with his daughters. They are the only women in the long enumeration. They are not to be forgotten. We have no idea how many daughters Shallum had, only that it was more than one. Later translators tried to expunge them by calling them "sons" but the Hebrew is clear. The daughters have been given back to us in more recent versions and they belong there to remind us that women played a role in one of the greatest building enterprises ever undertaken.

Fifty-two days later, a wall built by enthusiastic amateurs, with gates that could be
closed nightly against an enemy, stood for all
the world to see. Since there were few trained
masons the walls might have leaned a bit
askew and the bolts might have turned with
difficulty, but Jerusalem could again lift her
head to the world and announce: "I am once
more a city."

None of the exhausted workers could have
surveyed the completed project with greater
satisfaction than the daughters of Shallum.
Women had left their mark on the new Jerusalem.

~MARY OF NAZARETH~

If these daughters of Shallum are found
among the last pages of the Old Testament
the most reverberative "yes" of all opens Luke's
gospel in the New Testament. It belongs to
the woman who stood at the moment in history when heaven and earth came together.
She was poor and she was known to God
alone, and her "yes" will change everything that
is to follow.

It is hard to peer through the mists of
time and art and mythmaking to find the real
woman who was Mary of Nazareth. Yet we
must try if we are to understand anything of
who she is. It is a delicate operation because
our individual faith journeys intersect here

with a first-century world, and it is confusing. What can we say with certitude?

Mary was certainly young, quite poor, and in the first stage of her marriage to a wood and construction worker named Joseph. In this stage of espousals, we are dealing with more than a modern engagement. It is a binding marriage. Should either partner die, the other would be considered widowed. However, they did not yet live together. When he had finished their living quarters, usually an addition to his father's house, the spouse would come to claim his bride and the living together time of their marriage would begin. Mary and Joseph were not yet there.

Matthew's gospel makes clear that Joseph's family line goes back through David to Abraham, so he comes from the "right stuff." The legitimacy of a child depended upon his father's naming or claiming him, so Matthew makes sure that the reader knows that it is to Joseph that God's plan is revealed, it is to him that the child's name is given, and it is Joseph who, after the briefest of birth scenes, "until she had borne a son," names that child; so, in the eyes of the world, this is Joseph's child. All this is as it should be in the realm of the Mosaic Law.

Luke is writing for a different audience and from a different perspective. He is most probably not a Jew and his audience is that huge Gentile world that cares little about the niceties of Davidic kinship. This is a world waiting for the Good News that the poor too might be part of God's plan. Luke does this with a glorious sense of drama. He opens his gospel in the splendor of an evening offering in the Temple in Jerusalem, a time when Zechariah is greeted by an angel come to tell him that his prayer has been heard and he will be the father of John the Baptist, whose ministry will be far from the ritual and majesty of temple worship as he is destined to prepare the way of the Lord.

With an artist's eye, Luke then shifts from the panoply of Jerusalem to a tiny village in the northern part of the country, Nazareth, where Mary is living as she waits for Joseph to complete their living arrangements. We have to discard the fairytale stories of her parents bringing her as a child to grow up in the Temple (there were no arrangements there for little girls to be housed and educated). Mary is almost certainly poor, as was everyone in Nazareth. She is a village girl, carrying water with the others from the town well, going to the market, making use of the village oven, most probably, making her plans for her future with Joseph.

He too is a village boy, regardless of his ancestry. It is hard to believe that her parents would have arranged Mary's wedding to the decrepit old man from much of Christian art. No, he would have been a few years older than she, but not decades older. After all, he has to live long enough to care for her and the family they would have.

On a given day, when Mary is busy with her ordinary activities, Gabriel comes into her life with God's idea. Mary is perplexed, confused, and quite willing to ask the equivalent of "Why me?" Whatever plans she had had for that day, they are no more. Israel has been longing for the Messiah for centuries, and this fervor was especially real in first-century Palestine. The wives of high priests and officials all prayed their expectations, but we doubt that Mary did. What qualifications did she have?

God sends to ask if she might be willing to take on this task. To sit with that is to be as confused as Mary must have been. In a whirl of doubts and disclaimers, one thing is clear. If this is what God might want, she is willing to be a part of it. "Here am I, the servant of the Lord; let it be with me according to your word." Her "yes" is for no plan or idea of her own. It is simply for what God might want her to do. How complex and how selfless is her openness.

Mary is ready to trust God with the details, ready to launch into the darkness of what has never happened before, ready to go on without a contract or a plan of daily details for raising the Son of God. There is no way to know all that tumbled through her mind when Gabriel took his leave. She clings to the news that her cousin Elizabeth too was with child, and Mary heads south to find her and spend some weeks with her as the lives of their children take root and grow within them.

The next months are not easy. God seems slow to get in touch with Joseph about the fact that this child is of God. When the birth draws near, there are no reservations for a proper birthplace. We would have done better than to drag this couple all the way south to Bethlehem, only to find no shelter except one fit for animals. The poverty of the birth and the uncertainty of the future remind us that Mary's "yes" is not an assent given once and then all is well. It becomes a daily part of her living. It is not for one day only but for all those of the life of Jesus entwined with hers.

There are so many unmarked moments as we dig a bit deeper. When does Jesus begin to know who he is? Does he confide in her as to how he would shape his mission? As he grows up and takes direction from Joseph about construction and woodworking, what does Mary think? When these men of her family go off to the synagogue on the Sabbath to hear the prophets speak of the One who was to come, what goes through Mary's mind?

She is a strong woman, so much sturdier than the wispy virgins of art, so much more real than the royalty with which the Renais-

WOMEN WHO SAID "YES"

sance painters endowed her. She wore no crown or any clothing different from the plain tunics of all women. She is one of us, the most glowing example of a truly liberated woman whose God waited upon her word.

~THE BENT-OVER WOMAN~

It is Luke who provides us with another glimpse of a woman whose "yes" yields such benefits. In 13:10 we have one of the more delicious encounters of Jesus with his implacable enemies. It is the Sabbath and Jesus is teaching in a synagogue. Luke writes: "Just then there appeared a woman with a spirit that had crippled her for eighteen years. She was bent over and quite unable to stand upright."

Can you see her? Today we would have treated her for osteoporosis or some bone disease. In that world she was seen as in the grip of evil, each year bending closer to the ground, hobbled by Satan himself. How does she find her way into this synagogue, which is a masculine world for the healthy non-sinner? She is disqualified on all counts.

We do not know if she has decided on her own to seek out Jesus or if she has been planted there by the enemies of Jesus to see if he might violate the Sabbath and do the work of healing her.

47

As soon as she is perceived a space grows around her. No one wishes to touch her, even inadvertently. Jesus sees her, and calls her to him: "Woman, you are set free from your ailment." There is no way in English to translate that "woman" but in Hebrew it is a term of great respect. This is the first step in her healing. The second occurs when Jesus lays his hands upon her. He did not have to do this. His word alone would have made her whole. But it has been a long time since anyone dared to touch her, and the gesture of Jesus bridges that gap in her life.

She straightens up to her full height and the first thing she sees is the smiling face of this rabbi whose hands are on her shoulders. She begins to praise God. How could she not? The horrified synagogue leader makes a pulpit announcement that borders on the hilarious. He announces that one should come on one of the other days of the week for healing. Work should not be done on the Sabbath. He keeps repeating it, trying to be heard above the hubbub of joy as the townspeople hail this little woman's wholeness.

Since this was a village synagogue, almost certainly it was not open on any other day. These peasant farmers and tradesmen were at work long before sunrise. Only on this Sabbath day did they have time to come to their gathering place.

Jesus, however, sees the malice behind the proclamation. He calls the congregation "hypocrites," actors, or pretenders. He then points out the truth that no matter what the day, Sabbath or ordinary workday, each of them has an animal that must be untied and led to a water source. There is thunder in his voice as he proclaims, "Ought not this woman, a daughter of Abraham...be set free ...on the Sabbath day?"

For an instant, the congregation is shocked into silence. Have they heard what he just said? Every Jewish male prided himself on being a "son of Abraham," the first of those who believed in the word of God. They and they alone carried the faith from generation to generation. Women had no part in that. It is a male prerogative. Jesus corrects that by teaching through this woman that women too can live and act as believers.

The gospel notes that his opponents are put to shame as the entire crowd rejoices. They surely follow this woman, who stands as tall as she can, as she steps out into the street, looking up at treetops that she has not seen in almost two decades, drinking in the beauty of the bougainvillea climbing the walls, smiling as a camel crosses the road.

All the external joys now available to her are as nothing to the sense of self Jesus has given her: she is one worthy to be respectfully addressed, she is free, and she belongs to the great Abrahamic family. Her soul soars as she says "yes" to every gift Jesus has given her this morning, gifts that heal more than a body too long bent under physical suffering.

~3~

WOMEN WHO SAID "WHY NOT?"

RUTH; THE MEDIUM OF ENDOR; THE WOMEN PATRONS; MARTHA AND MARY; THE CANAANITE

Life is not always so simple that an affirmation or a rebellion is the best answer. There are times when the more doubtful "why not?" is the best one can summon. Biblical women find themselves in the same kinds of quandaries that we do. Looking at their situations offers food for thought.

~RUTH~

The incredible little book of Ruth somehow found its way into the Bible right after the discouraging text of Judges, when Israel was more intent on following its own way than on listening to God. In Ruth we are given a picture of a family at the end of the

Iron Age, somewhere in the eleventh century BC. The first verses are not hopeful. Famine has struck Bethlehem, and Elimelech has gone to live in Moab with his wife, Naomi, and two sons.

We miss the horror that those words would have struck into the hearts of the original audience. Moab was a traditional enemy that had long before failed to meet Israel's needs as the tribes came out of Egypt toward the Land of Promise. The Moabites were cursed as a result, and none of them was to be admitted to the assembly of the Lord down to the tenth generation. (Deuteronomy 23:4) To go to live among them was to admit to total failure.

More sad news follows. Elimelech dies, his two sons marry Moabite women, and then they too die. In a picture of absolute misery, by verse 5 we are left with the widowed Naomi and two widowed pagan daughters-in-law, Orpah and Ruth. There are no male survivors. With nothing more to lose and word that the famine had eased, Naomi decides to go home to Bethlehem, and the two girls agree to accompany her. She gently tries to dissuade them.

To go with her is to give up all hope of a future marriage, and it is to go to a foreign land where they will have no place. Orpah listens to her practical words and goes back but there is no dissuading Ruth. Has her family rejected her for marrying a man of Israel? Perhaps. Does she feel a sense of obligation to this older woman whose son she had married and loved? Perhaps. Does a future in Bethlehem seem more desirable than one in Moab? Perhaps. All we know is that she refuses to turn back and she lays claim to Naomi, declaring that her people and her God belong to Ruth as well.

Back they come, a depressed and bereft Naomi and a determined Ruth. Since they have nothing and it is harvest time, Ruth takes on the role of the poor and goes to glean in the ripe fields. This was a time-honored practice — to allow the poor the dignity of work. The Bible is very careful to note the instruction that no owner of a field is to reap to the edges nor are his gleaners to go back for what might not have been ripe on first picking. (Leviticus 19:9)

Ruth is soon noticed by the owner of this field, Boaz, who has come to supervise. When he inquires about her, he is told that she is Ruth the Moabite come back with Naomi. The entire second chapter never fails to name Ruth without adding "the Moabite" as if to stress her foreignness. Boaz is struck by her and gives orders to leave some grain standing for her to pick. He also puts food and water at her disposal and orders the young men not to molest her. When she asks why, he replies that he has heard what she is doing for her mother-in-law. As a result, Ruth brings home an abundance of grain and Naomi perks up enough to inquire how this has come about. Into the darkness, comes a shaft of light. Boaz is kin. He might want to be their kinsman-redeemer or next-of-kin.

This title could be of great importance in a tribal world. If a man died without children, his brother bore the responsibility of marrying the widow and naming the first son for the deceased husband. This guaranteed that his name would not die from memory. If he were the eldest son, then there was land to be acquired as well.

In the case of the widowed Ruth, there are no brothers to take on this role, so it shifts to the nearest male relative and it seems that Boaz has a prominent place here. Of course, the obstacles are very real. Ruth is a Moabite, one from a despised race. Is Boaz brave enough to take her as wife? There is only one way to find out.

That night, Ruth approaches Boaz, who is sleeping near the threshing floor to guard the new harvest from marauders. In the darkened granary, attired in her best, she dares to lie at his feet, pulling the edge of his cloak over her. This is her request to be taken under his protection. She boldly says, "Spread your cloak over your servant, for you are next-of-kin."

The startled Boaz agrees and blesses her for her actions in providing for her mother-in-law. He would like to follow through on her proposal of marriage, for that is what it is, but there is another kinsman, more closely related, who has the first right of refusal. Boaz promises to see to the matter as soon as the sun rises and Ruth goes home to report to the delighted Naomi that things are in motion.

True to his word, Boaz goes to the city gate and waits for the nearer kinsman to come by. He invites him to sit down while ten townsmen are gathered as witnesses. Boaz then proposes the acquisition of Mahlon's land, which the kinsman would love to have, but he balks when he is told that the childless Ruth is part of the bargain. He cannot do it since he is in the process of setting up his own family.

Boaz, in the presence of the ten witnesses, acquires the property and Ruth the Moabite. The townsmen bless him with prayers for fertility. Those prayers are answered for Ruth does conceive and bear a son, Obed, who in his turn has a son, Jesse, who has a son, David. A pagan Moabite, unafraid of entering a foreign land where she will be enemy, unafraid of asking for what she most needs, unwilling to abandon a widowed mother-in-law, has thus worked her way into the royal line of Israel and into the ancestors of Jesus.

Energetic, adventuresome, willing to believe that would-be enemies could be kinsmen-redeemers, Ruth is an amazing character to emerge from this Iron Age situation. However, her willingness to risk all finds its counterpart in a later character, one who comes to us without a name.

~THE MEDIUM OF ENDOR~

She is known only as the Medium or the Witch of Endor. In 1 Samuel 28, she is found at an almost hopeless time in the last days of the reign of King Saul. Aging, having squandered the goodwill of his people in a long-running attempt to kill David, and now facing a battle with the relentless Philistines, Saul is at the end of his rope. He attempts to "inquire of the Lord" but there is no response from a God he long ago abandoned. He no longer has a prophet he trusts and he is desperate, so desperate that he turns to his servants and says, "Find me a medium."

That isn't hard. She is in the village of Endor. What might she have thought as a knock sounds on her door and three strangers step in out of the dark? She does not recognize the king and she senses a trap when Saul asks her to conjure up a spirit, so she carefully sounds him out. "Surely you know what Saul has done, how he has cut off the mediums and wizards from the land. Why then are you laying a snare for my life to bring about my death?"

Saul protests that no harm will come to her. She hesitates, sensing that her life is hanging in the balance. If it is a trap, she is dead. If she refuses, she is alone at night with three strangers who can slay her. She must have decided it was worth trusting the word of the leader as she asks, "Whom shall I bring up for you?"

Saul asks for Samuel, the last of the judges, the man who had anointed him as king and the one who had told him he had forfeited the monarchy. Up from the shades a spirit rises. (We must note that at this period in Israel, there was no firm belief in life after death. The dead were in Sheol, a shadowy place beneath the earth from which they could be called forth by those with the correct power.)

As the woman sees Samuel's spirit she cries out, "You are Saul." The king reassures her and begs her to tell him what she sees. When she describes an old man wrapped in a robe, Saul falls to the ground before the specter, who rather querulously asks why he has been disturbed. Saul bravely puts his questions to him. "What shall I do as I am surrounded by the Philistines and God has turned away from me?"

He is honest in his query and Samuel is equally honest in his blunt reply that defeat in battle will be his on the morrow and that Saul and his sons will join Samuel. The spirit disappears and the king collapses, full-length, on the ground. He had eaten nothing that day and the thought of what lies ahead is more than he can bear.

At this moment all the motherliness in that medium rises to the fore. She insists that the king have some food so that he might physically face what is to come. Overriding his objections she has him sit on the edge of her bed while she slaughters the fatted calf and bakes unleavened cakes for him. Saul's last meal comes from a woman who has risked her life to give Saul a message he would rather not have heard. The brutal message and the loving meal end this scene.

We have no idea if this woman is an Israelite or not. Her profession had been outlawed, but she risks her life to do what she feels called to do. That takes courage and she follows through when she discovers that it is the king himself who is standing in her hut. She has no shame that she does not live better nor does she hesitate to minister to a petrified ruler who faces certain death. She has no chair to offer him but she can feed him from her larder. It is her food that carries Saul into battle and to his death on Mount Gilboa the following day. She slips back into history, still nameless.

~THE WOMEN PATRONS~

What might she have thought of women in another period of time who were equally ready to risk all? We meet them as Jesus begins his teaching life in public. These are part of the group that Luke speaks of in 8:1–3.

We are told that as Jesus made his rounds of the villages of Galilee, he was accompanied by the twelve and by "some women" who had been cured of evil spirits and infirmities. We need to remind ourselves that all sickness in the biblical world called for isolation. The communicable and the contagious, the chronic and the incurable, were all lumped together by a population that understood little of illness. All came from "evil spirits." Thus, the restoration to health was to be celebrated as a release from the power of evil.

However, this group of women is not just a thankful band. They answer a practical question. How did Jesus eat while on the road? Who shopped and cooked for the group? The answer is here in this "quartermaster" corps that cared for the practical side of Jesus' ministry. What an intriguing lot they are.

The first named and thus probably the most influential is the very controversial Mary of Magdala. What are the facts of her life? She came from Magdala, a small town on the western side of the Sea of Galilee. Because of its location it is believed by most scholars to have been a flourishing place. And the "seven demons" from which she had been freed? They have no relationship to sin; they are synonymous with disease or illness in most cases. Thus, we can conclude that she had been a very sick woman, healed by Jesus. She took her resources on the road with her — was she a wealthy widow or the only heir of a rich merchant? We do not know. All we know for certain is that she had money.

We have to remind ourselves that this study is limited to the texts of the universally accepted books of the New Testament. There are, of course, other avenues where we might find Mary of Magdala, particularly in the gnostic gospels and in their fictional spinoffs. None of them is being examined, probably to the regret of some readers!

In them we might find Mary in many guises, from that of wife of Jesus, to his lover, to the founder of a Jesus dynasty. Some of these are provocative ideas and some are preposterous, but they do not fall within the scope of what we are considering here.

One persistent error must be touched upon, however. For too long history has identified her as a prostitute. There is absolutely no scriptural authenticity for this. She is not the woman of the previous chapter of Luke who was "a sinner." This mistaken identity plus the exuberant art of the Middle Ages has fixed Mary in too many minds as the town harlot. No, Mary had been a very ill woman who was made well and who gratefully put her money at the service of the mission.

She is joined by the intriguing Joanna, who appears nowhere else in the Gospels. She is a married woman, wife of the chief steward of the household of Herod. This ruler is in the process of establishing a new capital in the freshly built city of Sepphoris, and one can see his right-hand man, Chuza, here, there, and everywhere as northern Galilee bustles with possibility. How did he so generously fill his wife's purse and permit her to follow this itinerant rabbi? Was he a secret disciple? Was his wife doing what he could not? We will never know his motivation but he has to have approved of her activity.

Susanna remains with us as a name only. There are no biographical details, but the early Church valued her action enough to make sure her name appears. If this is tantalizing so is the phrase "and many others" that follows. We long to beg Luke to elaborate, but he does not.

What we must do is include them in our mental pictures of Jesus teaching, healing, and traveling across Galilee. A faithful group of women is always part of the scene, listening, learning, even as they plan the next meal and take turns with the shopping. Domesticity and theology go hand in hand for a group of women who must have excited some commentary in the villages where they traveled. They are doing what women did not do. They are disciples of a rabbi. Luke records no critique of their actions but they cannot have passed unnoticed as they created a new role for women.

~MARTHA AND MARY~

Were they the inspiration for Mary of Bethany? Possibly. In another badly misunderstood passage of Luke, we meet this Mary in chapter 10:38–42. She and her sister, Martha, live in Bethany, one of the tiny villages in the hills overlooking Jerusalem. They must have been old friends of Jesus and on this day he stops there for a meal. The dialogue that follows has a familiarity that tells the reader that this is not his first visit.

Martha is busy doing what she does best, preparing a meal for this large group. We can see her peeling vegetables, stirring what is in her pots, when she catches sight of what her sister is about. Mary is sitting at the Lord's feet and is listening to what he is saying. The phrase "sitting at the feet" of anyone is not a posture. It is making a claim to discipleship. Mary is doing something that women did not do in the first-century world.

Martha is most probably skilled in her kitchen and the meal that she will produce, if served with love, will be worth the wait. That is not Mary's gift. She is struggling to find what is better for her. Martha is a bit horrified at Mary's audacity. She is even more anxious since in that outdoor world, the arrival of Jesus has probably attracted some of the neighbors. What will they think? And so, she bustles up to Jesus with her complaint: "Lord, do you not care that my sister has left me to do all the work by myself? Tell her to help me."

The reply of Jesus has been misunderstood by countless readers. Jesus gently rebukes Martha as he calls her by name. He also puts his finger on her problem, "You are worried and distracted by many things." It is a kind way of telling her to care for Martha first. He cannot tell Mary to give up her listening and head for the kitchen. Instead he uses an enigmatic phrase: "Mary has chosen the better part, which will not be taken away from her." Better for whom? In this instance, since Jesus must want his supper as much as the next person, Jesus seems to be telling these sisters that each has the right to claim her way to serve.

So Mary dares to lay claim to educating herself with the words of Jesus. This is a liberation moment for each woman and a challenge to the idea that there is only one way to bring one's gifts to the kingdom of God. Jesus is freeing them from the rules of a society that had fixed the place of women. Mary's daring is not without its price.

We only meet these sisters one other time, in a different gospel and a different situation.

John's gospel, in chapters 11 and 12, lets us see them at the time of the death of their brother, Lazarus. It is apparent that together they have sent the message to Jesus about his illness, but it is the ever-energetic Martha who leaves the mourning house to meet Jesus on the road and to challenge him for not having come sooner to heal his friend.

In the dialogue that follows it is so clear that Martha has done much thinking as she has worked in her kitchen. She and Jesus speak of faith and of eternal life. It is to Martha that Jesus says, "I am the resurrection and the life." And it is Martha who goes back to the house to bring Mary to Jesus, who waits on the road. All three go together to the tomb of Lazarus and Jesus calls him back to life.

Chapter 12 has the too often overlooked sequel to this raising of Lazarus. Of course, the sisters must celebrate and so a dinner party is prepared at which Martha serves. No meal could have been prepared with greater love. That is not Mary's gift, so she goes to her room and seizes a bottle of pure nard, one of the costliest of perfumes. (If the price indicated in the gospel is true, it is worth ten months' wages for a workingman.) We know that she pours the whole thing out on Jesus' feet, in a wildly wasteful gesture of love that Jesus will defend.

Food well prepared, a pound of nard given away — each sister has said her "why not?" about the gift given. We cannot separate these two women. They are each and all of us as we struggle to find our gifts and use them in service.

~THE CANAANITE~

One of the most daring of seeking women is found in Matthew's gospel in chapter 15: 21–28. Jesus has left the region around the Sea of Galilee and has climbed the mountains to set foot in the pagan territory of Tyre and Sidon. Since this is the only time he leaves the land of Israel, we have to be alert to what follows.

He has no sooner arrived than a woman in need begins to shout out to him, "Have mercy on me, Lord, Son of David; my daughter is tormented by a demon." Matthew calls her a "Canaanite," a term of derision that dates back more than eleven centuries to the oldest of Israel's enemies. Is this just to emphasize what an outsider this pagan is? She might be that, but she uses messianic terminology to address Jesus on behalf of her sick child.

For some reason, Jesus seems not to hear her and the nervous disciples appeal to Jesus to send her away. If we needed anything to convince us of their immaturity, this incident is it. Why don't they send her away themselves? They cannot take the initiative.

Jesus finally answers that he has been sent only to the lost sheep of the house of Israel. This is the opening the woman has been waiting for. She now approaches him and kneels before him with a simple, "Lord, help me."

Jesus still resists and it is hard to discern what tone of voice he might have used for his reply to her. "It is not fair to take the children's food and throw it to the dogs." ("Dog" is still a Mideastern word for any outsider, appearing on signs at the entrances of mosques to keep foreigners out.)

This nimble-minded outsider will not be put off by that. Her retort is both humorous and true: "Yes, Lord, yet even the dogs eat the crumbs that fall from their masters' table." She has succeeded because Jesus praises her: "Woman, great is your faith! Let it be done for you as you wish."

As she disappears down the street to her home where a healed daughter awaits her, we are left to puzzle over this strange little incident. There are several possibilities to consider. Is she the one who persuades Jesus to extend his table to the non-Jews? Or has Jesus come here to teach the disciples a lesson that faith is not limited to Jewish males alone? Does he know all along what the end result will be, but he tests her faith first so the disciples can witness it?

It remains a puzzle, despite several sign-posts: First, Jesus certainly undertakes this journey for a reason. Since he seems to leave almost immediately, the disciples must have asked themselves, "Did we come all this way for that?" Second, Jesus calls her "woman," that term of enormous respect that he uses in rare circumstances. Third, how has she heard of him and of his powers? She is miles away from Galilee, beyond some rugged mountains. Where did she acquire her faith?

We cannot leave her without another look of admiration at this pagan woman, from an undesirable people, whose love for her child is so great that she will not be repulsed by the whining disciples or by their master who is anything but encouraging. With nothing to lose, she acts on her "why not?" and leaves us a startling example of persistence in faith.

~4~

WOMEN WHO SAID
"WE MUST"

DEBORAH AND JAEL; ATHALIAH; PHOEBE; PRISCILLA; LYDIA

There are not always alternatives. While we sometimes lament when it seems there are too many choices, acting can be equally difficult when there is only one difficult road to follow. In this chapter, we will look at women whose choices were limited but who refused to sit and do nothing. One of them is less than admirable, but she is nonetheless a woman of conviction.

~DEBORAH AND JAEL~

We begin in the eleventh century BC, in the book of Judges. We have referred to this strange little book before. It comes to us from the bleak Iron Age, when Israel had lost its way and was governed by judges, tribal leaders who played both military and civilian roles. Each is introduced by the phrase "Israel cried to the Lord for help," usually after having fallen into idolatry and being attacked by enemies. The Lord always hears the Israelites, raises up a leader to deliver them, and, after a brief period, they again relapse.

In this manner, in chapter 4 of Judges, we meet the only woman judge, Deborah, who is introduced to us as both a prophet and the wife of Lappidoth. Her place to transact business is beneath a palm tree in the hill country of Ephraim. This presents an interesting scene.

Israel cries out for help since King Jabin, its enemy, is assembling his nine hundred iron chariots. Deborah summons the army commander, Barak, and tells him he is to take up a position on Mount Tabor so that he might sweep down on the enemy general, Sisera, who will be at the Wadi Kishon below. God promises to deliver the enemy into Barak's hands. Victory is assured.

But Barak demurs. Looking straight at Deborah, he proclaims, "If you will go with me, I will go; but if you will not go with me, I will not go." Some scholars suggest that having a woman as judge is already a sign of Israel's weakness. To hear an army general this defiant does not bode well for the courage of the conscripts.

Deborah does not hesitate. She will go to battle with him, but she assures him that the glory of the day will not be his. A woman will dispose of the enemy, Sisera.

Both sides make their preparations. Sisera has enormous self-satisfaction as he assembles his iron chariots, weapons of mass destruction such as no man had ever before seen.

Deborah gives the call to battle from Mount Tabor and Barak leads the charge down to the wadi. The battle scene is poetically described in chapter 5, in one of the earliest pieces of dramatic poetry we have. It tells us that in the heavens the stars fought for Israel and that Kishon became a raging torrent. That is an important fact. The wadi was one of those innumerable dry riverbeds that only had a function in the rainy season to help with the runoff from larger streams.

On this day as the rain poured down, Sisera's nine hundred chariots are literally stuck in the mud, unable to turn their wheels, and the mighty general is forced to flee on foot. He heads for the nearest shelter and thinks himself in luck when he spies the tent of Heber the Kenite. The Kenites were not allied with Israel; they were ironworkers, and it is possible that some of them might have worked on the building of the ill-fated nine hundred chariots. However, this might also have been forced labor, which their families resented.

It is that possibility that could account for the actions of Heber's wife, Jael, the only person at home on this day. She comes from her tent with a welcome, "Come aside, my lord, turn aside to me; have no fear."

The exhausted man stumbles into the tent with gladness. She covers him with a rug and gives him some warm milk to drink. A bit revived, he is still the general giving orders, and he tells her to stand at the entrance of the tent and to deny to passersby that anyone is within.

Jael smiles and says nothing. Does she harbor resentment for the way her husband and his tribe have been treated? No one knows. She quietly removes a tent peg, takes it into the tent, places it over the temple of the now sleeping Sisera and nails him to the ground. Then she waits outside the tent.

In a short time, Barak comes by in pursuit of the enemy who has so terrified him. Jael goes to meet him and invites him to come and see the man he is looking for. Israel is again delivered from the hands of the enemy.

The power of ancient poetry is fully alive in the battle hymn of triumph that follows this narrative chapter. Deborah is hailed as a mother in Israel before the poem settles into the rhythms of a marching army. Then Jael, the tent-dweller, is also blessed for her plotting in dramatic terms: "he sank, he fell, / he lay still at her feet; / at her feet he sank, he fell; / where he sank, there he fell dead."

The anonymous author then shifts perspective to another woman, the mother of

Sisera, who is awaiting her son's return from battle. She is anxious at the delay and tries to think of excuses so as to reassure herself, one of the most human of occupations. She finally comforts herself, as she peers up the road through her latticed window, that he is busy dividing the spoils of captured women and embroidered cloth.

We are left with two chapters of feminine triumph, of a woman marching side by side with her general to the battlefield, with a courage that he lacked, and of another woman who used trickery to make certain that the enemy did not get away. Deborah and Jael are unforgettable.

~ATHALIAH~

A woman can use her strength for good or for ill, depending on her circumstances. An intriguing example of a woman who plots for evil is to be found in 2 Kings 11. We are in the middle of the ninth century BC, and the Kingdom of David has long dissolved into a northern and southern set of territories, each jockeying for power and for the favor of God. It is a time of bloodshed, of naked grabs for power, and of assigning God a place in the background of a dusty Temple.

The northern part of the country, now known as Israel, is in the hands of Ahab and his notorious queen, Jezebel. (We shall meet her later.) The southern part, known as Judah, is governed by Joram and his queen, Athaliah, daughter of Jezebel. Thus she comes as a foreigner into the country, but she is not shy. She has brought her god Baal with her as a rival to the God of Israel.

When her husband dies, she remains in power as queen mother during her eldest son's rule. At his death, she makes her move. If there are no royal heirs, she will wield undisputed power. She gives the order to destroy the entire royal family. These are her children and grandchildren who are ruthlessly killed. What she does not know is that, in the chaos, her sister-in-law, Jehosheba, has stolen away with the tiny prince Joash and his nurse. She manages to keep his whereabouts a secret for six years in an inner room of the temple compound, no doubt with much help from the high priest and other good people of Judah.

Were there royal functions when Athaliah and Jehosheba crossed paths? When a devotee of Baal and a faithful follower of Yahweh saw each other heading for different temples and smiled politely? Did the queen dismiss the other as part of the past while, she, Athaliah, belonged to this new day? The possibilities are endless.

The drama of chapter 11 takes place six years later when the day has come for the coronation of the tiny new king. He is now seven, and he is brought into the Temple courtyard, where the guard has been carefully assembled. The crown is placed on his head and he is given the covenant (a scroll of the Bible?). As the glad shout goes up from every throat, "Long live the king," Athaliah hears the clamor and comes to see what is transpiring.

She sees a child, her grandson who should be dead, standing crowned in the midst of a tumult of joyous people. She tears her garments in grief as she screams "Treason! Treason!" But the treason is hers and her execution is ordered, although not in the Temple. She is led out ignominiously through the horses' gate to her death.

Her huge grab for power ends in failure since she reached too far and too ruthlessly. Did she never sense the growing opposition during the six years that the high priest and his allies spent waiting for the child to be of age? Had her absolute rule blinded her to an increasingly restive people? One would love some insight into her ideas on leadership vs. domination.

~PHOEBE~

If Athaliah dared to do what she thought was possible, the New Testament offers intriguing glimpses of women who found themselves called to lead in formerly unheard-of ways. In the first years of a post-Easter Christian community, the majority of the believers were Jews who faithfully continued to worship in the Temple and synagogues as they always had done. To this they added a gathering on the first day of the week, in memory of the resurrection of Jesus. Where would they meet?

Almost naturally, they found their way into each other's homes. Since they were re-membering what Jesus had last done with them, they gathered for a meal. In this way, the women of these first communities be-came the natural hosts, welcoming the group, setting food before the guests, and offering a new kind of leadership.

We have no orderly records of this period, only the idealized glimpses in the book of the Acts of the Apostles and the casual references in the letters of Paul. These, however, are sufficient to see that women easily became the focal point of the house churches.

It is here too that Paul's leadership is vital. He sets up these churches, praises the women who welcomed both him and his fellow Christians, and pleads with the larger church to do the same. His Letter to the Romans 16:1–3 offers a tantalizing glimpse of this new role for women.

Paul has seemingly put this letter into the hands of Phoebe, "a deacon of the church at Cenchreae…" He calls her "our sister," the common family term used by the early church for female believers. He then says that she is a deacon, not a "deaconess," as some translations would have us read, nor a "servant," as others translate it.

Cenchreae was the port where ships going from Athens to Corinth would stop. Standing on its landing place one can look straight down the road to the distant mountaintop of Corinth. This was a bustling, busy place, and the Christian community here would not have been insignificant.

Phoebe has an official position in it, and Paul uses that to introduce her to a church group that does not know her. He also adds that she has been a "benefactor of many and of myself as well." Does she represent the next generation of those women who financed Jesus' ministry? It is delightful to consider this woman of some means and prominence in a city whose docks were lined with goods from around the world. She tucks Paul's letter into her bag and sets off to deliver it to a group of Christians who do not find it strange that a woman has this task.

~PRISCILLA~

Why would they when they have already accepted new roles for women in this new Christian world? Many of them would know Aquila and Priscilla, working and traveling companions of Paul who were in the process of rewriting what women could and could not do. We find this couple in the book of Acts, chapter 18.

From the details here we are told that Aquila is a Roman Jew exiled by order of Claudius. This allows us to date the incident as occurring in the year 49 AD, the year when the Emperor Claudius had expelled Jews from the city of Rome when he suspected them of rioting. Aquila and his wife must have been caught up in this purge and so made their way to Corinth. Since they are leatherworkers, they readily find a way to make their living. Paul, being of the same trade, takes them as congenial work partners and fellow Christians. He comes to rely on them as together they spread the Good News in the tumultuous city of Corinth.

They seem to work in the morning and teach in the afternoons, with Paul seizing every Sabbath opportunity to speak in the local synagogue. When he is rejected there, he makes his way to the house of a believer next door, and carries the message to the Gentiles. After eighteen months in Corinth, Paul moves on to Ephesus in Asia Minor and Priscilla and Aquila go with him.

It is in Ephesus that the eloquent Apollos makes his appearance. We are told that he is well versed in the scriptures, but knows "only the baptism of John." That puzzling phrase seems to indicate that his indoctrination into

Christianity is incomplete. Who is to teach him? Priscilla and Aquila take him aside and more accurately explain the Way of God. It is interesting that she is named first, that both she and her husband are teachers, and that the learned Apollos does not find this inappropriate. This is a new role for women.

Paul makes further mention of this husband-wife team at the end of Romans when he says of them that they "risked their necks for my life, to whom not only I give thanks, but also all the churches of the Gentiles. Greet also the church in their house." (Romans 13:4)

~LYDIA~

In the wider Greco-Roman world outside of Palestine, women seemingly had no difficulty moving into these new positions as leaders and teachers in the Christian communities. In this regard, we cannot overlook Lydia of Philippi whom we find in Acts 16: 11–40. She is in a category by herself!

She is unique for several reasons. In the story of Paul's early journeys as an apostle, he has largely confined himself to Asia Minor. Everything shifts in chapter 16 when, in a vision, a man from Macedonia invites him to "come over." Those words read easily but what is happening is that Paul is being invited to leave provinces whose customs and ideas are more or less familiar to take the word of God to mainland Europe, to Greece itself. Philippi is the first city of any size in Europe where Paul and his companions stop to preach.

It was a Roman colony on the Via Egnatia, built as a new city to lure the veterans of Rome's wars to settle there, with financial incentives, and so to insure the Roman influence near an important highway. Paul is not surprised to find no synagogue there so, on the Sabbath, he goes to the riverside, knowing that Jews often gathered in such places when they lacked their own house of prayer.

To his surprise, Paul finds no Jewish men, but rather a gathering of women who worked for Lydia, a dealer in purple cloth. We are told that she is "a worshipper of God." She also has to be fairly successful as a businesswoman since purple was the emperor's own color and its use was carefully restricted. Roman senators got a band on the bottom of their tunics. Other mortals could only hope for an imitation brownish-red dye that came from the madder root. True purple came from the crushed shell of a small crustacean in a painstaking and costly process. Lydia's "household" seems to be a group of women who assisted her in this enterprise.

They gather round Paul and Luke to listen eagerly to what these men have to say, after which they ask for baptism. Then Lydia invites Paul to come and stay at her home. The text adds, "and she prevailed upon us." Wouldn't one like to meet the woman who could prevail upon Paul of Tarsus?

That does not end Lydia's role. Paul and his companions stay on in the city and end up getting arrested and dragged before the local magistrates on trumped-up charges of disturbing the peace. They are rushed off to prison where they spend the night singing hymns and praying, until an earthquake strikes, and the jail collapses. The jailer is ready to kill himself since he presumes all those under his jurisdiction have escaped. A dust-covered Paul calls out that they are all there and he has nothing to fear. The man asks for baptism on the instant and takes his former prisoners home for some first aid.

The magistrates, in the meantime, have rethought Paul's arrest — did they discover that he was a Roman citizen who could not be so condemned without a trial? We do not know but they send for Paul, telling him he is free to go. He refuses, demanding an official apology. When this is offered, in person, he still is not ready to head for the highway.

Paul goes to Lydia's house, where he encourages the brothers and sisters gathered there. She has seemingly become the head of that first European Christian community and the fact that she is a businesswoman is not a deterrent. While she never again enters the scene of activity, the letter Paul will later write to the church at Philippi is quite special. It is one of the most tender, most positive to come from his pen. He concludes by congratulating the Philippians on their generosity to him from the earliest days of the gospel. Lydia must have well laid this foundation stone.

In the face of opportunity these women each consider the possible paths before her and then make a choice, most for good and one for ill. None of them allow fear of the unknown to paralyze her.

~5~

Women Who Said "We Challenge You"

Tamar; Jezebel; Herodias; The Anointing Woman

It is readily apparent that the women of the Bible are not meek bits of the background in a very active male world. If we dig a bit deeper we find some women who challenged authority at the risk of their very existence.

~Tamar~

The first of these comes to us from Genesis 38. That early in the patriarchal story we meet one of the sons of Jacob, Judah by name, who has left his ancestral lands and gone to live among the Canaanites. This in itself does not bode well and when he soon marries a Canaanite woman we are uneasy.

The text tells us that their firstborn son, Er, is named by Judah, but the two boys that follow are named by his wife. That is contrary to custom. Is he somehow rejecting those two?

As a father, Judah does his duty and finds a wife for his firstborn, a woman named Tamar. The young husband dies before his wife has a child, so Judah tells the second son that he is to marry Tamar, and name the first child for his dead brother, an accepted custom. He rebels and dies himself soon after. That leaves Judah, once rich in sons, with only one unmarried boy and no desire to offer him to the unlucky Tamar.

Instead he violates all accepted practices and sends her home to her father as an undivorced widow to await the day when the third son will be ready for marriage. This puts Tamar in a kind of no-man's-land. Her father cannot arrange a new wedding for her nor can she get on with her life as a widow. She is free-floating in a world of careful categories.

How long she has to wait we do not know but the third boy comes to manhood and there is no change in her status. Judah's wife passes on and when the mourning period ends he feels the need for some social activity. He accepts an invitation to come to Timnah for sheepshearing. This is all Tamar needs to hear and she leaps into action. Her widow's garb is stripped off and she wraps herself in a large veil before finding a place on the road to Timnah where Judah must pass.

He sees this person by the roadside and judges her to be an available prostitute. She asks what he will give her and he promises a kid from the flock. Has he spoken to his daughter-in-law so few times that he doesn't even recognize her voice? She pretends not to trust his word and asks for a pledge to be held until the goat arrives. When he reciprocates by asking her to specify what pledge, she asks for his signet, his cord, and his staff. These are the signs of his identity, his manhood, and his position as a head of household. Judah cedes them without demur.

She then lies with him and they both go on their way. Judah later asks a Canaanite friend to take the kid he promised to that prostitute by the roadside and to reclaim his pledge objects. The friend tries but no one has ever heard of such a prostitute. An embarrassed Judah decides not to pursue the matter since making it public would make him look the fool. He has given away his birth certificate and his driver's license, by today's standards.

Within a few months, Tamar's pregnancy becomes known and it is reported to Judah. He is indignant since she is his property, as it were, and now she is damaged goods. He condemns her to death, but to a death unheard-of for her crime. He condemns her to be burned.

As she is being led to execution she sends a package to her father-in-law with the words, "It is the owner of these who made me pregnant." He opens it to discover his signet, cord, and staff. Fully ashamed, Judah halts the execution and confesses, "She is more in the right than I, since I did not give her to my son Shelah."

When the time of her delivery comes, Tamar gives birth to two sons, as if in recompense for her two dead husbands. When Matthew compiles his genealogy to open the first gospel, Judah is there, but so is Tamar as the mother of the boys. This quite gutsy, ingenious pagan woman is an ancestor of Jesus himself. She is wryly humorous, inventive, and determined to have her rights. In that she succeeds.

~JEZEBEL~

Another pagan woman, equally determined but in very different circumstances, is found in 1 Kings 18. Her very name sends a chill down the reader's spine since Jezebel has become synonymous with evil and plotting. She comes into the Bible from the small northern kingdom of Sidon to become the wife of King Ahab of Israel.

A bit of history will help our focus here. The kingdom of David and Solomon had split into northern and a southern countries, Israel

and Judah. Since most of what we have about
Israel was written from the southern perspective, it has a negative slant. What we read
about Jezebel was written by her enemies.

To be fair, she probably looked upon this
marriage as a step down from what she had
been accustomed to. She arrives from Tyre,
an island kingdom with two harbors on the
Mediterranean. Tyre was a great maritime
empire benefitting from trade with other
kingdoms. The wealth of the world had gone
its way. Jezebel's arranged marriage is a further attempt to extend the power of Tyre
since Israel controls the land trade routes to
and from the East.

Jezebel comes into a country that does
not even have an official worship site, since
the Temple now belongs to the southern
Judah. Ahab makes every effort to accom-
modate her by building a temple for her god
Baal. This sets up an immediate conflict between the monarchs and the active prophet of
God, who is Elijah. This Elijah even seems to
control the weather since he announces that
the drought in the land is punishment for the
people's abandoning the worship of God

As a famine ravages the land, the people
interpret this as further divine displeasure.
Jezebel begins an active persecution of the
prophets of the God of Israel and Elijah's
supporters by forcing most of them into hid-

ing. Elijah confronts Ahab who greets him, "Is it you, O troubler of Israel?"

It is indeed and Elijah retorts, "I have not troubled Israel, but you have." He goes on to challenge Ahab to assemble the prophets of Baal on Mount Carmel and they will see who has power.

In one of those scenes that the Bible paints so well, the mountaintop is crowded when Elijah arrives there. Four hundred fifty prophets of Baal face the solitary Elijah who thunders to the crowds of the curious who have gathered to see what might happen: "How long will you go limping with two different opinions? If the Lord is God, follow him; but if Baal, then follow him."

Everyone is silent. What can they say? Then Elijah proposes that the priests of Baal erect an altar, pile the wood of sacrifice on it, prepare a bull, but bring no fire. He will do the same for the God of Israel. Then each will cry out to his god and the one who answers is God indeed. It seems like a fair test.

The prophets of Baal go first, carefully preparing their altar and then beginning ritual prayers and self-slashing to attract Baal's attention. No fire appears.

Elijah taunts them, suggesting that their god might be meditating or on a journey; perhaps he is napping and must be awakened. The entire day passes and the altar remains in readiness with no fire to consume the sacrifice.

Then Elijah steps up and says, "My turn now." He directs that his altar be prepared as theirs was, but he pours water over the animal offering and the wood, once, twice, a third time. Then he stands and prays to the God of Abraham, Isaac, and Israel, asking for an answer so that the people might know who is God. In an instant, fire sweeps down from the heavens, consuming both sacrifice and altar itself, even licking up the water that had run off into the trench around the altar.

The enraged populace turns on the prophets of Baal to slaughter them, while King Ahab watches in amazement. Elijah continues to pray until a cloud comes out of the west as the prelude to a rainstorm that ends the drought. The king's chariot wastes no time in tearing back to the palace to let Jezebel know what has transpired.

She is infuriated and curses Elijah, declaring that she will see him as dead as the prophets of Baal before the next day ends. One is astonished at Elijah's reaction. He has just ridiculed her prophets and proven them powerless. He has reestablished the concept of God in the minds of the people, but a curse from this foreign queen and Elijah takes to his heels. He runs the length of the country and on into the Sinai desert, where he begs God to take his life.

But God is not finished with him yet. He sends food and drink to Elijah to give him strength for the journey and then leads him on to Mount Sinai with the question, "What are you doing here, Elijah?" God tells him that he is to go back because there is still work to do, but he rewards him with a vision of God himself passing by.

No, he is not in the thunder on the mountain, nor in the lightning, nor in the power of the earthquake. In an instant of sheer silence, God passes and Elijah's call to speak the truth is renewed. Back he goes, now accompanied by a helper in the person of Elisha. He will no longer be alone.

Jezebel is still exercising her power over her husband, Ahab, who comes across as both stubborn and spineless in a defining incident in chapter 21. He has decided to plant a vegetable garden, not the usual occupation of royalty, but he is stymied by Naboth, who owns the vineyard in the very spot where the king wants to plant his potatoes. Ahab offers to give him another place for his vineyard or its value in money. That seems fair to the king, but he is strangely ignorant of how his people see land.

Biblically, the land always belonged to God. Human beings had only the use of it, family by family, and could not treat it as we might real estate today. Naboth is raising grapes on ancestral land, which has to remain within the family. It cannot be sold to an outsider, even the king. Ahab does not get this.

Resentful and sullen, the king goes back to the palace, refuses to eat, and lies on his bed with his face to the wall. The queen finds him in this position. When she inquires if he is ill, he tells his little tale of the vegetable garden that cannot be. (The childishness of Ahab is most probably accentuated because these accounts were written by scribes from the southern kingdom and they are ridiculing the rebel country of the north.)

"Do you now govern Israel?" snaps Jezebel. "I will give you the vineyard of Naboth the Jezreelite." She then shows that she has well absorbed the niceties of the law of the land. She writes letters in Ahab's name and uses his seal to make them official. A fast is proclaimed at which two scoundrels are to denounce Naboth for having cursed God and the king. (The law of Israel required two witnesses to a crime.) Naboth was to be immediately removed from the assembly and stoned to death.

It happens exactly as she plans. Then Jezebel goes to Ahab and tells him to take possession of that vineyard for his planting. Obediently, Ahab does as she tells him, but he meets Elijah on the way.

Elijah minces no words, but lays bare the crime of Ahab, predicting that in the very spot where Naboth died, the dogs will also lick up the blood of Ahab. Elijah is equally unsparing in describing the future death of

Jezebel. Ahab seems to be struck by the dire words of Elijah and does penance, which earns him a brief reprieve. However, when he is mortally wounded in battle a few years later, his blood is washed from his chariot at the very spot that Elijah had predicted.

Jezebel is still alive, no doubt guiding her two sons during the next fourteen years. She never deviates from the two guiding principles of her life: the absolute rights of an oriental monarch and her devotion to her god Baal. We have to wait until 2 Kings 10 to witness her death.

By then Jehu has seized power by slaying Jezebel's second son and he is furiously driving his chariot toward the palace where she is residing. She knows that she is doomed so she plans to face her death with the same strength of will that she has shown elsewhere. In 2 Kings 10:30, she puts on her makeup for the last time, attends to her coiffure, and takes her place at a window. As Jehu comes through the gate, she calls down, "Is it peace, murderer of your master?" One has to admire her final defiance.

Jehu calls up to the palace eunuchs, "Who is on my side? Throw her down." They do so as Jehu drives his horses over her body and enters the palace for his celebratory meal. During this he reflects on the callousness of his actions and tells the servants to see to her burial "for she is a king's daughter." They scurry to obey him, but they are too late. The wild dogs have torn apart her body, and all that remains is Jezebel's head, hands, and feet.

Scholars have recently begun to wonder if these remains are not the result of her carefully adorning herself for this encounter. If she had used henna, a common practice in her day, the bitterness of that plant would have kept the dogs from touching the parts of her body where it was. Whatever the reason, Elijah's prophecy about her demise is fulfilled.

With a shudder, we turn from her story, but one cannot help but be struck by the incredible force of character of this pagan woman whose influence on her husband and children have given her name lasting fame. She challenged everyone and everything that stood in her way, and went to her death with defiant courage. She is not to be ignored.

~HERODIAS~

Nor can we ignore the New Testament woman whose name too is forever linked with the ugliness of power wielded wrongly. Herodias steps from the pages of Matthew's gospel in chapter 14 with an attitude not too different from Jezebel's.

The complex story of the Herodian dynasty gives her her place in an entangled web of family marriages and murders. Suffice it to say that this dynasty originated in a desert tribe that saw opportunity on the horizon with the rise of the power of Rome and prepared for it by converting to Judaism. When the Roman legions arrived in Palestine in the first century BC and looked among the inhabitants for a client king, the family of Herod was ready. The Jews never accepted them as really representing the people of God, but the Herodians managed to cling to power for more than a century.

It was a century in which they married often within the family line and spouses were divorced and murdered with impunity. The family tangle is made more complicated by the naming custom in which "Herod" was given again and again. A family chart is necessary to comprehend fully all these complexities, but for our purposes we need only concentrate on Herod Antipas of the third generation, ruling in Galilee during the lifetime of Jesus and the monarch whose story includes that of Herodias.

She was initially married to a half-brother of her father and bore him a daughter, Salome. Herod Antipas seems to have come for a visit and wooed Herodias until she left her husband and married Antipas, also her uncle. The marriage was scandalous, and when the royal entourage takes up residence in a summer palace near the Jordan River, they are within reach of the ministry of John the Baptist.

We have no knowledge of how the two encountered each other, but John's judgment of Herod's situation is uncompromising. "It is not lawful for you to have your brother's wife." After all, this puppet king is claiming to be a Jew and such actions are forbidden by the Law. Herod dares to arrest him, but he fears public wrath if he has him put to death, so John is languishing in one of his dungeons. Mark's gospel adds the interesting note that "he liked to listen to him." (6:20) Did Herod go down to the cells at night to visit this outspoken prophet? It is Mark too who tells us that "Herodias had a grudge against him and wanted to kill him." She is forced to wait for her opportunity. It comes on the night of Herod's birthday banquet.

This was clearly a men-only party for Herod's officers and courtiers and the leaders of Galilee. The daughter of Herodias is invited in to dance for them, to the great pleasure of all present. Herod praises her lavishly and declares that he will give her whatever she asks for, even half his kingdom. He has clearly celebrated far too well, since his kingdom is not his for the giving. It is Rome's. However, the wild words have been said and the young dancer seeks her mother to help her formalize her wish.

Herodias could not have been more delighted. "Ask for the head of John the Baptist on a platter." Even Herod is aghast, but he had given his word and the gruesome trophy is brought to the girl, who takes it to her mother.

Herodias might have felt she had silenced her enemy, but this act only further antagonizes the population. John's disciples take his body away for burial and then they bring the news to Jesus, who withdraws to grieve his cousin's death.

One cannot help wondering if this sad little story is not behind Luke's account of Good Friday morning, when Pilate, looking for a way out of condemning Jesus, hears that Jesus is from Galilee and sends him to Herod, who is in Jerusalem for the festival. Luke notes that Herod "had been wanting to see him for a long time." (23:8) If Jesus and John were cousins, two men of roughly the same age and familial line, might they not have resembled each other? Was Herod anxious to prove that Jesus was not John come back to life? The only way was to see for himself, to question him and to hear that voice he thought he had silenced. But Jesus does not play his game. He remains silent, and Herod is frustrated.

Herodias uses her daughter to achieve her ends. This one scene is the only gospel reference to this arrogant woman, who is sensitive to criticism about her irregular lifestyle and is not willing to recognize any truth but her chosen one. Power and privilege are hers, but they lead to nothing productive.

Each of the first three women in this chapter, Tamar, Jezebel, and Herodias, chooses to find a way to change her situation when circumstances seem against her. Luke's gospel gives us another woman who seeks a new life.

~THE ANOINTING WOMAN~

In Luke 7:36–50, we find Jesus in a not unfamiliar situation. He has been invited to dinner by a Pharisee and has already taken his place at table. It seems as if this meal is taking place outdoors in the courtyard of Simon's home. The meal has begun when a nameless woman comes in from the village, carrying an alabaster jar of perfume. She is bold, to invade the masculine space of a meal. She is wealthy since alabaster jars of perfume were not available to the poor. She has a problem, as we see from her actions.

She approaches Jesus, who is probably eating in the Roman fashion on a dining couch. She kneels, begins to weep and, as her tears touch his feet, she uses her unbound hair to wipe them away, immediately anointing his feet with the contents of her jar. Then she respectfully kisses his feet.

The appalled host says to himself, "If this man were a prophet, he would have known who and what kind of woman this is who is touching him — that she is a sinner." Is this our clue that she might be the town prostitute? It could account for her wealth used for the perfume; it could also account for his unwillingness to accuse her or Jesus in too loud a voice. These dinner guests could be some of her "clients."

Jesus cuts through his dilemma with an offer: "Simon, I have something to say to you." This would ordinarily mean a rabbi had a story to share. Simon says, "Teacher, speak." Jesus tells a little parable of a man with two debtors, one owing a huge sum of money, the other a small amount. He then forgave them both. Jesus pauses and asks, "Which will love him more?"

Simon hesitates before replying. There must be a trick in this that he is missing, but, since he cannot find it, he slowly says, "I suppose the one for whom he canceled the greater debt." He must feel better when Jesus nods and says, "You have judged rightly."

His relief is short-lived, however, since Jesus then outlines Simon's deficiencies as a host. Jesus was not greeted, as he entered, by a servant with water to wash the dust of the street from his feet. He points to the kneeling visitor who has washed his feet with her tears. Simon offered no kiss of greeting; she has kissed his feet. Simon did not anoint his head with the customary drop of perfume. She has perfumed his feet. By now, Simon must be squirming on his couch. We will never know why he was so rude, since his purposes in inviting Jesus are never revealed. This woman upsets everything.

Jesus concludes with a triumphant: "Her sins, which were many, have been forgiven. Hence, she has shown great love."

There is a murmur at the table as the guests ask each other, "Who is this who even forgives sins?" Jesus lets them wonder without a reply. He turns his attention back to the anointing woman who is waiting. He has not yet spoken directly to her, but he does so when he dismisses her with, "Your faith has saved you; go in peace."

Still holding her jar, she gets to her feet, and walks out into her new life. She has actually publicly renounced her old one. One has to imagine the faces of her former customers. Whatever was is finished. She is new and Jesus has confirmed it.

That dinner gathering is the talk of the town that evening. So is this forever nameless woman who decided one day to change her way of living. She is an interesting addition to those who challenged the use of power for ill or, as in her case, for good. She faces the religious leaders of her village in a situation she creates and she wins the freedom to become new.

6

WOMEN WHO FOUND THAT "TWO IS TROUBLE"

SARAH AND HAGAR; RACHEL AND LEAH; PENINNAH AND HANNAH

The biblical story begins in an era so different from what we know. As Abraham walks into history around the year 1850 BC, it is a time with many givens that no one would think to challenge. Foremost among these is the very makeup of society.

In a largely nomadic world that revolved around tent living and traveling at the pace of grazing animals, women cannot be expected to have either the aspirations or the possibilities of women in our society. It was accepted as the norm that every woman would be married as soon as she reached childbearing age, that she would bring children into life, preferably sons, and that her life would be submerged in the goals and desires of her husband. We cannot judge it. We can only make note of it.

Life apart from kin was unthinkable, both socially and economically. A solitary woman had no way of supporting herself, so every set of laws we find in the ancient world makes some kind of provision for the unfortunate widow. There were not many of these. Most women died from childbearing long before their husbands. Again, these are simply facts.

~SARAH AND HAGAR~

Abraham walks out of ancient Mesopotamia and begins a long journey to the Land of Promise, a journey on which he is accompanied by family, a nephew and a wife, Sarah. She is given few words. They are not needed since he speaks for her.

In Genesis 12:10–20, we can catch a glimpse of this in action. The nomadic Abraham finds himself on the borders of Egypt, and he fears lest he be slain and his beautiful wife taken from him. He plots therefore to pass her off to the Egyptians as his sister. He tells Sarah that this is the plan. She is given no way to protest. At first, all goes well. She is taken into Pharaoh's harem, and Abraham is rewarded with gifts of livestock and slaves. Then disaster strikes.

Plague breaks out among the Egyptians, who investigate to discover a possible cause. When the truth is revealed about Sarah, an understandably angry Pharaoh expels Abraham from his country, but does not ask for the return of his gifts, these being presumably tainted. This is important since verse 16 mentions female slaves in the midst of livestock. This is how Hagar enters the story.

By chapter 16 Abraham is fairly well settled in the land of Canaan, but Sarah has borne no children. She takes the initiative in offering her slave, Hagar, to Abraham so that a child might be born. By the custom of the day, if the man then named this child, it was his heir and this surrogate wife would be considered as having given him new life and hope when his wife could not. Hagar does become pregnant, but her fertility causes a further problem.

Sarah accuses Hagar to Abraham of looking with contempt on her. This is very possible. In the confines of tent life, a concubine achieving what the wife could not might well be a cause of friction. It could also be a false judgment on Sarah's part. We have no way to know. All we know is that Sarah asks Abraham to resolve the impasse. He refuses with a scornful, "The slave girl is in your power. Do to her as you wish."

Sarah does. She treats Hagar so harshly that the Egyptian runs away, down into the Sinai desert, where she is found beside a spring. In the first annunciation to a woman in the Bible, an angel of the Lord (always a substitute for God himself) finds the despondent slave there and calls her by name, telling her to go back to her mistress. This message is amplified by the angel's revealing the name she is to give the child, Ishmael, and something of the wild strength that will be his. Hagar responds by naming God — that is, she calls this God of her master El Roi, "the God who sees," since he has seen her in her misery and has given her hope. It is amazing to have a record of a pagan slave daring to call the god of her master by a personal name.

Hagar must have fulfilled the angel's directives because we are told that when the child is born, Abraham names that son Ishmael, a name he could only have learned from her having shared it with him. The baby now bears Abraham's name and is his legitimate heir.

Life again becomes complicated for Hagar when Sarah later does get pregnant and bears her own child, Isaac. The very sight of Ishmael playing with his little brother so agitates Sarah that she again asks Abraham to act and he does, in a most unmanly fashion. (Genesis 12:8–21) Hagar and her child are driven out of the encampment, down into the wilderness of Beersheba.

After her food and water are gone, Hagar places her son in the shade of some bushes, and sits down to die. She cannot bear to look on her dying child. At this poignant moment, an angel again comes to her aid, pointing out a well that will give them both life. We are told that Ishmael grows up in this wilderness, acquiring the skills necessary to do so and, when the time comes, his mother finds a wife for him from the land of Egypt. She had never lost her contacts there, it seems.

Sarah lives out her life without another woman sharing her tent. At her death, Abraham does something most unusual. He goes to his Hittite neighbors and asks to buy land from them for her burial place. (Genesis 23) They offer to give it to him but he insists on paying for it. The Hittites then set a price and Abraham acquires a cave in a field, a place that will become the burial site of the three patriarchs and their wives. This is the first bit of land that the Chosen People will own in Canaan, and it is for a woman's burial.

Many years later when Abraham dies (Genesis 25:9), his two sons, Isaac and Ishmael, bury him beside her. In the genealogy that sums up this period Ishmael's descendants are named first, all twelve of his sons, which would indicate abundant blessings on the son of the slave girl.

Nothing comparable happens to Isaac. It will only be his grandson who is so blessed. However, that fruitfulness also involves more than one woman and a new visit to a polygamous tent.

~RACHEL AND LEAH~

We have already met Isaac and his exuberant wife, Rebekah, in chapter 2, when she so gladly traveled many miles to wed him. They are rewarded with twin sons, Esau and Jacob, whose sibling rivalry is the stuff of legend.

Esau is the elder and so the heir of his father, whose favorite he becomes. Jacob, less inclined to the outdoor life and hunting, is his mother's darling. There comes a day when Esau, fresh in from the fields, smells the odor of the stew his brother is cooking and begs for some. Jacob says, "First sell me your birthright." Esau does so, eats the savory dish, and thinks no more of it. (Genesis 25:29–34)

Legally, what has transpired has no reality. Birthrights cannot be sold, and Esau probably saw it as Jacob's putting a value on his fresh lentils. He dismissed it from his mind. But Jacob, whose name has connotations of trickery or supplanting, kept this memory warm.

Time passes and Isaac fears that, as his sight is failing and he is growing feebler, death might be near. He calls Esau and asks him to go hunting for wild game and to prepare a savory dish for him. Then he will bless him with the words a father reserves for his firstborn son. Esau happily shoulders his bow and arrows and goes out into the wilds. Rebekah has overheard her husband's request and decides the time is now to advance her Jacob. (Genesis 27)

She commands him to go to the flock and bring in two young goats. She takes Esau's best tunic and tells Jacob to put it on, to take the dish and go in to his father and get the blessing. Jacob says, "My brother Esau is a rough-skinned man and I am smooth. If my father feels me, he will know I am not Esau and I will earn a curse, not a blessing."

Rebekah is ready for that. She takes the goatskins and covers his hands and the nape of his neck. Then she thrusts the dish of meat into his hands and sends him into his father's presence.

The startled Isaac asks, "Who are you, my son?"

"I am Jacob, your firstborn. I have done as you asked. Now eat of my game, that you might bless me."

When Isaac questions the speed with which he found a wild animal, Jacob smoothly lies that the Lord had granted him success. Still doubtful, Isaac asks him if he is really Esau and he answers in the affirmative. Isaac has him come near and as he embraces him, he feels for his hands and touches their roughness. That and the scent of Esau in the borrowed tunic finally convince the blind father.

Jacob is blessed with the dew of heaven and the fertility of the earth, with grain and wine in abundance, and with the promise that nations will serve him. There is nothing more that a son could desire. Jacob escapes back to his mother, and Esau soon enters his father's tent bearing his savory dish. The heartbroken father realizes he has been duped, but there is nothing more to be given. Jacob has it all. Isaac can offer Esau only life in a desert far from home.

We see here the power of the spoken word. What is said cannot be unsaid. There are no lawsuits for impersonation or for theft of goods. The blessing is given. Jacob is rich and Esau is impoverished. The very angry Esau swears vengeance, and life in that camp is unpleasant. Rebekah swings into action again. Jacob must go into exile.

She directs him to go north to her brother Laban in Haran and to stay there until such time as Esau calms down. If he does not go, she fears for the life of Jacob, so angry is Esau. As a cover story, the journey is made to seem as if Jacob is in search of a wife who is not one of the local Hittite women. Off he goes.

One night as he nears the border of his homeland, Jacob lies down to sleep and has a strange dream of a ladder reaching from earth to heaven, a ladder populated by traveling angels. He hears the Lord tell him that this land will one day be his and that his heirs will live on it. On awakening, Jacob is awed, but still calculating. He promises that the Lord will be his God, just as he has been the God of his father, but first God must meet some conditions!

In one of the strangest of prayers he lays out what God has to do to earn this distinction. God has to help him travel safely, have enough to eat as well as clothing to wear, and then bring him safely home again to his father's house. Then, and only then, will he offer God one-tenth of all his goods. Thoroughly satisfied with himself, Jacob resumes his travels.

At the village well of Haran, he meets his uncle Laban's daughter, Rachel, for the first time. It is really love at first sight. After he rolls aside the stone that covers the well so she can water her sheep, he identifies himself and is invited to Laban's house. His visit there culminates in his striking a bargain with Laban. Jacob offers to serve him for seven years if he might marry Rachel, the younger daughter in the household. Laban agrees: "Better that I give her to you than that I should give her to any other man; stay with me."

The Bible here adds the phrase: "So Jacob served seven years for Rachel, and they seemed to him but a few days because of the love he had for her." (Genesis 29:20) If our story ended here, all we need add would be a "happily ever after" phrase. But this is not the end. Conniving Jacob is about to tangle with a father-in-law who is also a plotter.

There is another daughter in the household, Leah, who is older and has some physical impediment. In words that have stumped the translators, Leah's eyes are described as "light" or "lovely." Whatever is intended, Leah has not yet been married, so there seems to be some difficulty in finding a willing partner.

None of this is on Jacob's mind as he sits among the men at the wedding feast. (The women seem to have been elsewhere.) Evening comes and Laban brings the veiled bride into Jacob's dark tent. It is only in the morning light that the bridegroom turns his head and looks directly into the strange eyes of Leah, not Rachel, who is lying beside him. The trickster has been outtricked!

An infuriated Jacob roars out of the tent, "What is this you have done to me? Did I not serve you for Rachel? Why then have you deceived me?" (Genesis 29:25)

Laban calmly informs him that it is not the custom in the country to give the younger in marriage before the elder. He has the audacity to propose that Jacob finish out the wedding festivities for the rest of the week, and then, in return for another seven years of service, he can have Rachel too. Jacob agrees to acquire the second wife, but how much is concealed by the phrase "he loved Rachel more than Leah."

Life in this polygamous tent could not have been easy, and it is complicated by the fact that Jacob has sexual relations with both sisters. Leah is blessed by bearing son after son, each with a portentous name. For example, the first is Reuben: "Surely now my husband will love me." The second is Simeon: "Because the Lord has heard that I am hated, he has given me this son also." Four times, Leah gives him a son, but four boys do not seem to change her status from unloved wife.

Rachel is envious and accuses Jacob of failing to do right by her. She gives him her handmaid, Bilhah, so that she might be her surrogate. The maid is blessed with two sons, one after the other. Leah, afraid of losing out in the family race, offers her maid to Jacob also, so two more boys join the ones already crowding the home.

Jacob seems to have lost interest in Leah, so young Reuben helps his mother by collecting mandrakes in the fields, and bringing them to her. (They were believed to be a cure for infertility.) Rachel sees what he is about and asks for some of them. In a poignant exchange between the two wives, Leah says, "Is it a small matter that you have taken away my husband? Would you take away my son's mandrakes also?"

They bargain in typical Mideastern fashion. Rachel gets some mandrakes and Leah gets Jacob for the night, a night rewarded by yet another son. He is not the last. Leah has one more, plus a daughter, before Rachel finally has her day.

"Then God remembered Rachel, and God heeded her and opened her womb." (Genesis 30:25) Her barrenness is no more, and she gives birth to a son whom she triumphantly names Joseph, from the root meaning "may he add more." The stigma is gone and she can hold up her head beside her more blessed sister.

Jacob, meanwhile, observing his two wives, two concubines, and eleven sons plus one daughter, decides the time has come to strike out on his own. However, he owns no flocks. All belongs to his father-in-law and he has to find a way to acquire for himself. He prepares a plot. We can only wonder why it took him so long!

He goes to his father-in-law and asks for his wages. The wages proposed seem paltry. Jacob asks only for the speckled or spotted goats and the black lambs. Laban must have chuckled inwardly. These oddities of the flock are few and Jacob is going to end up with very little, he thinks. He doesn't compute Jacob's ability to trick.

Having removed his little flock from Laban's holdings, Jacob sets to work. He carefully peels sticks from the poplar and almond trees so that they are striped. When the flocks come to the watering places in the mating season, he places these rods before the most choice of the animals. Amazingly, that year the robust ewes all have speckled lambs, and the more feeble ones have normal offspring. Jacob's holdings increase exponentially! So do his problems.

Laban and his sons are furious but cannot figure out how they have been tricked. Jacob is smart enough to know that he is no longer welcome among his in-laws, but he needs some allies if he is to depart. He sends for both his wives and asks them to meet him in the fields, out of earshot of the household.

In Genesis 31:4, Jacob lays out the problem. He tells the two women that he has been cheated by their father and that his wages have been withheld, but that he, Jacob, has managed to acquire a large flock of speckled and spotted animals. Now he wants to go back to the land of his God, someone he has not spoken of much during these long years. He is implicitly asking Leah and Rachel to abandon the land of their gods and go with him into the unknown where an angry brother is still living.

The reply of the two wives is astonishing. They must have discussed this and, over the years, seen what their father had done with them. There is anger in their answer: "Is there any portion or inheritance left to us in our father's house?… for he has sold us, and he has been using up the money given for us." (Genesis 31:15) They are ready for a new life far from the man who turned their spouse into a kind of perpetual slave.

When sheepshearing time arrives, Jacob makes his move. Laban and his sons are far from home, but Jacob has been left behind. Is this a further indication of his lack of status? At any event, he packs up wives, concubines, children, and livestock and off they go. Unknown to him, Rachel snatches her father's household gods and puts them in her saddlebag.

The unwieldy company moves slowly so it isn't hard for Laban to catch up with them. He puts on the greatest pretense of sorrow as he complains of not having had the opportunity to send them off with festive music nor could he kiss them farewell, they, his sons and daughters. He saves the real reason he has come for last: "Why did you steal my gods?"

The genuinely perplexed Jacob invites him to search the campsite for anything that is his. Laban does, going from tent to tent, his fury most probably growing as he comes up empty-handed. He comes into Rachel's tent where she is demurely seated upon her saddlebag. She makes her excuses for not rising, saying that the way of women is upon her. Since this makes her ritually unclean, Laban dare not approach her.

When the search leaves Laban with nothing to show for his efforts, Jacob feels free to upbraid him, reminding him of twenty years of service honestly given and for what? He has been cheated despite his hard labor. Laban retorts that everything Jacob has is actually his — wives, grandchildren, flocks. That is an overstatement, which Laban probably realizes, so he suggests that they make a covenant between them to establish peace. On a mound of stones gathered by his children, Jacob promises peace and so does Laban. They part, once Laban has blessed the family he will never again see.

Two major events have still to mark this return of Jacob. The closer he comes to the borders of his homeland, the more he thinks of the wronged brother who must be waiting. When word is brought that Esau is en route to meet him, Jacob hurriedly divides his family into units, the concubines first with their children, then Leah with hers, Rachel with Joseph. Then, taking a deep breath, he walks forward to meet Esau.

Leah and Rachel, concubines and children, even the livestock hold their collective breaths as these brothers come together after a separation of so many years. They need not have worried. Esau tearfully embraces his brother and they exchange gifts before Esau proposes that they journey on together. He has a welcome prepared at his home for the brother he has forgiven. He seeks no revenge.

It is a strangely beautiful scene that these wives witness. Whatever they might have heard about Esau dissolves as they see his eagerness to reclaim this part of the family. Jacob is less trusting. Having just used trickery to escape his father-in-law, does he carry seeds of mistrust within him? Does he think back to his initial theft of the birthright and decide that he would not have forgiven? We will never know, but he sends Esau on ahead, promising to travel more slowly, at the pace of his children, until they will come to Esau's home where a welcome has been planned.

But no sooner has Esau left than Jacob chooses to turn westward, and he avoids the territory where Esau lives. There is no party that day.

Not too far along on the journey, shortly before its end near Hebron, Rachel's birth pangs come upon her and she gives birth to her second son. Sensing that she is dying, she proposes calling the child Ben-oni, that is, "son of my pain," but Jacob objects and names him Benjamin, "son of my right hand," or "much-loved child."

The little caravan pauses long enough to bury Rachel there, just outside Bethlehem where her tomb is still revered. Leah must have said her farewells to this younger sister with a certain sadness and finality. There was so much that went wrong in their relationship with the same man, but they had found common bonds before this great journey to a new land and Rachel will miss all that.

Leah herself is mentioned only once more, in Genesis 49:31. Many years and a lifetime later, Jacob is dying in Egypt, with an attentive group of sons at his bedside. Jacob gives final instructions for his burial and specifies that he is to be taken back to Hebron, to the cave where Abraham had buried Sarah. "There I buried Leah." Jacob might have been tricked into marrying her, might have loved her younger sister more, but it is Leah who has the final triumph by lying in the patriarchal tomb forever, far from the roadside burial place of Rachel.

~HANNAH AND PENINNAH~

The emotional hardships of polygamy are emphasized in the first chapters of 1 Samuel in the story of Elkanah and his wives, Peninnah and Hannah. The former had children, but Hannah had none. Each year when the household went to Shiloh to offer sacrifice to the Lord, as was the custom of Israel during the eleventh century BC, when the Ark of the Covenant rested in this place, the festal meal brought pain to the barren wife.

Each mother was given as many portions of meat as she had children to be fed. There was Peninnah with a large mound in front of her for all her sons and daughters, however many they were. The loving husband gave Hannah a double portion, but her rival still mocked her. Nothing could console Hannah, not even the tender words of Elkanah. "Why is your heart sad? Am I not more to you than ten sons?" In all honesty, his love did not atone for her failure in the eyes of the world.

So, on one of these visits, Hannah rose early in the morning and went alone to the tent that housed the presence of the Lord. There she weeps, as she prays fervently one more time for the blessings of motherhood. This time she vows that if the Lord grants her request she will dedicate her child to the service of the Lord.

She is being watched by the priest, Eli, who notices that her lips are moving but no sound is audible. Harshly judging her to be intoxicated, he urges her to reform her life. Hannah defends herself by sharing the reason for her anguish. Eli is touched and promises to pray with her.

Absolutely at peace, Hannah goes home with her rival and her husband, and, in due time, she becomes pregnant. Her prayer is answered by the birth of a son whom she names Samuel, from the Hebrew roots that are related to asking. This baby is indeed one who is an answer to her fervent request.

When he has been weaned, Hannah brings him up to Eli at the annual visit and leaves him there with the priest for the service of the Lord. "For this child I prayed; therefore I have lent him to the Lord; as long as he lives, he is given to the Lord." This incredibly generous woman wanted a child to establish her status as a good woman at a time in history when a child was just that sign. She must have held her head high as she offered him to Eli with a burst of joy that has long outlived its singer. She sings of the triumph of the weak and lowly whom God does not forget, a song that is at the heart of the one that Mary of Nazareth will sing in Luke 1:47–55. Separated by centuries, each one knows the power of God.

With the passage of years, she has three more sons and two daughters. Now Peninnah can gloat no more when it is time to serve the festive meal. Hannah has merited more than a double portion.

In a charming note, the text lets us know that each year she brought a new tunic to her firstborn son, presumably a size larger each year. Hannah's name is mentioned no more in the text, but her son grows up to become that pivotal character, the last of the judges of Israel, the man called up to anoint the first two kings of Israel, Saul and David. She could never have dreamed of this, but she would have found it a most satisfactory answer to her prayers. What mother could ask for more?

7

WOMEN WHO WERE TOLD WHAT TO SAY

ESTHER; MARY OF MAGDALA

The choice of words is not always given to a woman. Some are messengers, as it were.

~ESTHER~

In the book of the Bible that bears her name, we meet the remarkable Esther. Her story is presented as a kind of historical novel, set in the troubled Persian period of the fifth century BC.

There are problems with the text itself. The religious aspects are almost hidden and the name of God never appears in the Hebrew text. There are glaring historical inaccuracies and some clearly fictional details. The Persian king named in it and his spouse cannot be found in history. But, putting all this aside, the book of Esther offers the basis for the feast of Purim and gives us a woman of great courage who finds herself in dire circumstances.

In an opening chapter that could be a movie script we are introduced to a Persian king who is presiding over a magnificent banquet for his officials and all the governors of the provinces. The blue and white curtains hanging from marble pillars, the golden goblets, the huge flagons of wine, even the mosaic pavement, all present a picture of luxury and excess.

After six days of partying, while Queen Vashti was entertaining the wives of these officials, the king sends for his queen so that he might parade her beauty as part of the entertainment. For the occasion, she is to wear her royal crown to dazzle the intoxicated males. But Queen Vashti refuses to come.

The enraged king consults the lawyers to see what procedure he should follow. (The delicious account that is recorded is a wonderful mockery of the pagan Persians and their laws.) These wise men of the land report that this is serious business. If other women hear that the queen did not obey her husband they too might look with contempt upon their spouses. This cannot be allowed to happen so a royal decree is proclaimed: "All women will give honor to their husbands, high and low alike." When this is sent out, the king adds a note "declaring that every man should be master in his own house."

All this is the work of chapter 1. The reader is left with a picture of an irrational king, of wild excesses at court, and of a feisty little queen who is dethroned for refusing to become an object for a roomful of drunken guests. We now have a place for Esther to come upon the scene.

When the king's anger is somewhat abated, he realizes that he has no queen, so a search begins for a beautiful replacement. There will be a contest to collect the loveliest women from all the provinces. These will come to Susa for beauty treatments and then the king will make his choice.

All this comes to the ears of Mordecai, a Jew living in Susa, who has been guardian of his cousin Esther. Since she is an orphan, he has adopted her. This moment he sees might be his opportunity, so Esther becomes part of the group of contestants. Unknown to anyone concerned is her nationality.

After twelve months of beauty treatments, each young woman goes in to the king and then is returned in the morning to another harem. She would not return to him unless he calls for her by name. When it is Esther's turn she so delights King Ahasuerus (Xerxes) that he ends the contest, declares Esther queen, and sets the royal crown on her head. But we know that the story cannot end there.

Mordecai, her guardian, maintains his place near the palace gate for any news he might glean about Esther. One day as he lingers there, he overhears a plot to assassinate the king. He sends this news to Queen Esther. The matter is investigated and the perpetrators are hanged, all of which is recorded in the annals of the kingdom.

Further complications come from the rapid rise to power of a certain Haman, who is promoted by the king to a prime office that carries with it the honor of being bowed to whenever he is passed. Mordecai, bowing only to his God, omits this bit of honor and incurs the wrath of Haman. Haman decides that to punish Mordecai is too little. He will punish all of Mordecai's people by destroying the Jews.

Haman manages to get the king's ear long enough to convince him that the Jews are lawless and do not keep the king's rules so they should not be tolerated in the kingdom. He asks for a decree to destroy them all. The king's secretaries are called and the appropriate documents are written and promulgated, to the dismay of every Jew in Susa.

Mordecai, wearing sackcloth as do all his people, bewails the approaching death. He takes up his seat at the palace gate. When Esther hears of this she sends a messenger to find out the cause of his dismay. The messenger returns with a copy of the decree and with a charge to Esther that she must go and entreat the king for her people.

She responds by citing the Persian law that no one may approach the monarch without having been called by him. The penalty for such presumption is death. Mordecai sends back a stern answer to Esther that she is not safe in her harem. No one will escape the royal decree. He concludes with the words, "Who knows? Perhaps you have come to royal dignity for just such a time as this?"

Esther's reply is to ask that he have her people join her in a three-day fast. Then she will go to the king and "if I perish, I perish." The prayers of the Jews begin to rise to the Lord.

On the third day Esther puts on her royal robes and approaches the king, who is seated on his throne. When he catches sight of her he extends the golden scepter of his favor and asks her to name her request, anything she desires, even half his kingdom. The suspense grows since all she asks is that the king and Haman come to a banquet that she is preparing that evening. He is delighted to agree.

Haman is summoned and the two men come to her meal. When the king again asks what Esther might desire, she begs the two to come again the next day to a banquet that she will prepare and then she will make her request. They are both only too eager to agree.

Haman's high spirits are jarred when, as he returns home, he spots Mordecai at the gate and that despicable man still does not rise to bow before him. In some rage he goes to his house, summons his family and friends, and recounts his good fortune in having been twice summoned to a banquet hosted by the queen. Yet even this honor is spoiled by the stubborn Mordecai's refusal to acknowledge his, Haman's, position. What should he do?

His wife and friends have the answer. He should build a gallows fifty cubits high and in the morning he should tell the king to have Mordecai hanged on it. Then he will be free to enjoy the second banquet of the evening. Haman agrees with them.

In a wonderful bit of storytelling, the plots shifts to the palace where the sleepless king, seeking a cure for his insomnia, asks to have the annals of the kingdom read to him. When he hears about the plot to assassinate him that had been reported by Mordecai, he asks "and what reward was given this man?" The answer is that nothing was done for him. Aroused to action, the king asks if any royal official is up and about. He is told that Haman has just come into the palace.

That is all the king needs. He summons Haman and asks him what should be done for one the king wishes to honor. Haman has come to propose the death of Mordecai, but he puts that aside since he is sure that the king wishes to honor him. He boldly proposes that royal robes be given the man, that he should ride on the king's own horse, and that a royal official precede him proclaiming, "This is the man that the king wishes to honor."

The smile on his face must have disappeared as the king replies, "Go quickly and do this to the Jew Mordecai who sits at the king's gate." Haman has no choice but to obey. He goes back to his home disconsolate again and this time his wife wonders if this Mordecai is somehow destined to prevail. He has no time to plot again before it is the hour for the banquet.

Esther is now ready for her moment. When the wine has been passed and the king is in fine spirits, he again asks her to make her request, for anything, even half his kingdom. Esther pleads for her life and the lives of her people, saying that if the decree had been for banishment or enslavement, she would not have spoken, but this annihilation of her people will damage the reputation of the king too.

The bewildered and infuriated monarch realizes that he has signed a decree that he has not understood. "Who is he, and where is he, who has presumed to do this?" Esther says, "A foe and an enemy, this wicked Haman!"

The drama of the scene is intensified as the furious king goes out into the palace garden to think through his rage, leaving the terrified Haman with Esther. He throws himself on the couch where she is reclining to plead

for his life at the moment that the king returns and accuses him of assaulting her. Haman's fate is decided when a palace official
points out the waiting gallows and Haman is
hanged there.

The king holds out his golden scepter to
Esther, gives her and Mordecai the estate of
Haman, and tells her that she may write
whatever she pleases with regard to the Jews
in the name of the king, and it will be promulgated. Esther has saved her people.

In one sense, Esther is almost a pawn. She
has no power to make the first decisions that
put her in the palace and win her the king's
favor. We might question the wisdom of
Mordecai in so using her beauty. However, in
the moment of crisis, Esther is stirred by the
suggestion of Mordecai that all that went
before was for her to use at this time. She
does just that, with humility and courage, and
so becomes one of the heroines of Judaism.

~MARY OF MAGDALA~

To carry a message can be an act of courage, so we need to look at a woman centuries
later, in the New Testament, in chapter 20 of
John's gospel, when Mary of Magdala finds
her true purpose. We have already met her as
one of the material supporters of the mission
of Jesus. All that she learned there about discipleship comes to the fore here.

No gospel is totally clear about the actions of the women on Easter morning. The one thing they all agree upon is that, early in the morning, there are women on their way to the tomb to make certain that the burial of Jesus was proper. In the haste and horror of Good Friday two men had taken care of the arrangements, Nicodemus and Joseph of Arimathea. It was not safe for the women to wash the body and wrap it, with spices, in the burial cloth. The men did this.

In that long Sabbath day of grief and re-criminations between Friday and Sunday many words must have been spoken about human failure and fear. The women could do nothing on the day of rest, beyond buying the appropriate spices as soon as evening came. Then they had to wait.

What is amazing is that no one goes to the tomb in the hope of a resurrection. No one remembers that Jesus never spoke of his death without adding that on the third day he would rise again. No, no one remembers. The only visitors on Easter morning are there to perform more burial rites. That is the role of the women. No man has the courage to ac-company them this early in the morning on a day when Jerusalem is still a dangerous city.

They find an empty tomb and someone runs back to tell the male apostles, who come and verify this. Only men can witness to some-thing officially. When that has been done, the other women go back to Jerusalem too, and Mary of Magdala remains behind to grieve in this last resting place of her Lord.

As with many of us, when something has been lost we go back for a futile search of the same places where we have already looked. Mary does this too. She goes back to the empty tomb for another glimpse to see if she has missed anything. She hasn't. She is thinking, "They have taken away my Lord, and I do not know where they have laid him." Who she meant by "they" we do not know, but she is not seeking a Risen Jesus.

Still weeping, she does not seem the least bit surprised when Jesus himself appears behind her and asks, "Woman why are you weeping?" He adds, "For whom are you searching?" She is ready for this. Judging him to be the gardener, she asks that if he has carried him away, would he please tell her where he has put the body, and she will take him away. The words make little sense. Physically, she could scarcely carry the dead body of an adult male, but in the emotional state that has enveloped her, she could probably do anything. Jesus very calmly says one word: "Mary!"

To hear her name on his lips pierces that emotional fog and Mary now knows who he is. Her reply is one word also: "Rabbouni!" This is her teacher and she is ready for the lesson. Jesus needs her to convey a most important message to the male disciples barricaded in the Upper Room.

First he tells her that she need not cling to him since she will see him again. But she is to go to his disciples, all of whom failed to follow to the very end, and she is to say: "I am ascending to my Father and your Father, to my God and your God." He is letting them know that they are still in the family, that new family he worked so hard to establish. They have been forgiven and they still have the right to be God's children.

Can you imagine the effect when Mary went back to Jerusalem, opened the door where grief was still the prime emotion, and announced triumphantly, "I have seen the Lord." That must have caught their attention so that she could give the rest of the message. They do not know it yet, but he will come himself that evening to teach another lesson on forgiveness. But for the moment this word from Mary of Magdala changes everything.

They must have spent the afternoon remembering what he had said to them while he was still among them. They must have spoken of his death and resurrection. They must have shed tears of gratitude that he still wanted them for the work ahead. Did anyone ask why he had given this word to Mary? Was her place of leadership so assured that it was natural for her to be the messenger?

We can only speculate. All we know for sure is that the first post-Easter apostolic message was from a woman to a group of men, to Jesus' inner circle. It is a sign that all will be new in the kingdom.

~8~

WOMEN WITH WORDS TO CHANGE THE STORY

BATHSHEBA; ELIZABETH

We will never know what human pen chronicled the saga of David, who rose from shepherding to establishing the united kingdom of all the tribes of Israel. Whoever he was, he has left a set of rich portraits of an incredibly human ruler and of those who were part of his personal and his public life. Almost every chapter of the story that runs from 1 Samuel 16 through 1 Kings 2 reveals another facet of David and the men and women around him.

~BATHSHEBA~

The eleventh chapter of 2 Samuel begins like this: "In the spring of the year, the time when kings go out to battle, David sent Joab with his officers and all Israel with him; they ravaged the Ammonites, and besieged Rabbah. But David remained at Jerusalem."

That is all the reader needs to hear to know that trouble is afoot. Once the rainy season has ended, it is time for a little warfare, for a few battles to bring home booty and fill the empty coffers. Why would the king not go with his men? What will he do alone in his house with no male companionship? What David does is to get immediately into serious trouble.

He rises from his couch late one afternoon and strolls about his rooftop, which overlooks all Jerusalem. Down below, on a humbler rooftop, a very beautiful woman is bathing, unaware that the king is observing her. David makes inquiries and learns that she is Bathsheba, the wife of Uriah the Hittite. Centuries before, the Hittites had been a mighty world power. Now, its men were valued soldiers for hire by other world powers. Bathsheba was almost certainly a Hittite too, since the men rarely intermarried with other cultures.

David sends for her and she cannot refuse. There is no male at home to protect her, and David is well aware of this and of the fact that her husband is serving in David's army. He "lay with her" and then sent her home. Time passes and she sends word to the king's house, "I am pregnant." David begins to plot.

First he sends a messenger to the battlefield where his nephew Joab is in charge and asks to have Uriah returned to Jerusalem. When the Hittite arrives, David makes vague inquiries about the status of the war and then sends Uriah to his home. The loyal soldier remains in the courtyard with the other servants and when David questions him as to why he did not go to embrace his wife, Uriah explains that all the country is at war, even the Ark of the Covenant is in its tent. Who is he to embrace civilian life and its joys while his fellow soldiers do not have the opportunity for such happiness?

Foiled in his first attempt to cover up the source of Bathsheba's pregnancy, David asks Uriah to stay one more day while he compiles a message for the general. That night Uriah is invited to the king's table for dinner where every effort is made to get him drunk. Uriah still stays in the courtyard to sleep off his wine. He does not enter his house.

David readies his message for Joab. It is blunt and crude. Joab is to set Uriah in the forefront of the battle, and when things are at their most furious he is to draw back the support of the troops so that Uriah might be killed. The cold-blooded plan works, and Uriah dies. Once the mourning period has ended, David sends for Bathsheba and marries her.

This pathetic set of actions leads to one of the most dramatic encounters in the entire David story. Like many rulers of the period

David has his own prophet, Nathan, who comes to him one day to tell him a story. It is a little parable about a rich man who had flocks in abundance while his poor neighbor had but one ewe lamb that he had nurtured and raised with great love. When a visitor arrives on the doorstep of the rich man, he is unwilling to take an animal from his own flock, so he takes the lamb of the poor man and prepares dinner with it.

David's anger is roused and he interrupts Nathan to say, "That man deserves to die." Nathan's reply is, "You are the man." David is forced to face his sin and its consequences. A sad period follows in which the child falls ill and dies, despite David's fasting and prayers. In the mentality of the eleventh century BC, that has to happen. Then David rouses himself to start life anew and Bathsheba bears a second son, Solomon. It is this child who brings us to Bathsheba's only other appearance in biblical history.

David does not lack for wives — he has eight of them — nor for sons — there are at least ten. What he does lack is any succession plan. We might automatically think in terms of the eldest, but that is not necessarily how these kingdoms functioned. David's character is also a part of this complicated scene. He loves his family too much to either discipline or form them, so his family narrative features quarrels among half-brothers, fratricide, and

even a civil war led by the incredibly person-
able Absalom. All this culminates in a final
decisive scene engineered by Bathsheba and
her allies in the king's house.

"King David was old and advanced in
years; and although they covered him with
clothes, he could not get warm." (1 Kings
1:1) Into this chilly moment steps Adonijah,
eldest surviving son and eager to claim the
throne even before the death of his father.
Through Joab he has the army on his side as
well as one of the priests, so he decides he will
self-proclaim since he believes his father is
too frail to object.

Nathan is still active, still anxious that right
prevail before it is too late. He has also allied
himself with Bathsheba and the high priest,
Zadok. They make their plan and Bathsheba
comes to the throne room to present her request. She reminds David that he had promised that her son Solomon would succeed.
Now, she says, Adonijah is about to declare
himself king. It is time for David to act. If
not, when another comes to the throne,
Solomon and she will be outsiders and will be
put to death.

There is no way to know if what she says is
true or not. It sounds like the kind of thing
David would have promised this woman he
had so wronged. It is equally possible that she
and Nathan hatched this plot to foil the other
plotters. No one will ever know which version

is true. But it is her words that David considers as he sits shivering on his throne.

Nathan arrives to reinforce her request by protesting slyly that David had forgotten to tell him that Adonijah was having a feast before announcing his kingship. Why didn't the king tell him what was to transpire? David rouses himself, orders the royal mule to be brought round, and has Solomon ride it down to the Gihon Spring to be anointed while the trumpet is blown and he is proclaimed king. It is interesting that David makes certain that Bathsheba is in his presence when this momentous change is announced. He endorses her version of events.

The joyous shouts of the Jerusalem populace reach the ears of Adonijah's allies just moments before they are to make their own move for the throne. They are too late.

Bathsheba, not an Israelite, treated almost as an object in her original dealings with David when she is sent for and sent back home, given no voice in her pathetic situation, does indeed have the last word and a high place. We find her seated beside her son King Solomon in 1 Kings 2. We also find her in the genealogy that opens Matthew's gospel, one of the four foreign women who were the ancestors of Jesus. She continues the Davidic line that leads to him through her son. She spoke when it counted.

~ELIZABETH~

A thousand years later, in very different circumstances, another woman spoke. We meet Elizabeth in the first chapter of Luke's gospel, and her credentials are impeccable. While her husband is listed as belonging to the priestly line of Abijah, she comes from the family of Aaron, brother of Moses and the first high priest of Israel. Both she and Zechariah are righteous and of blameless life, we are told. All should be well, but…and that little word changes everything.

This seemingly good couple has no children. In the culture of the first century of our era that is a tragedy and it is the fault of the woman. To compound the difficulty, we are also told that "both were getting on in years." Since life expectancy was so much shorter then, they might well be middle-aged by our reckoning.

Elizabeth certainly lives with the disapproval of her neighbors. God must be punishing her for something. Let's underline that judgment by coming to the day when Zechariah returns mute from his duties at the Temple. How he conveys to his wife that he has seen an angel who has promised them a child, we do not know. All that is recorded is that Elizabeth does become pregnant, a joy that she keeps hidden for over five months.

Imagine her surprise when a visitor arrives on her doorstep in her sixth month of pregnancy. It is her young cousin, Mary, come all the way from Nazareth with a joy to share. Elizabeth's piety and her perceptive spirit are one as she greets her visitor, "Blessed are you among women and blessed is the fruit of your womb. And why has this happened to me that the mother of my Lord comes to me?" It is at this moment that the child in her womb leaps "for joy." It is a tender scene as older and younger mothers-to-be embrace with no one to witness except their remarkable but as yet unborn children.

Mary stays with Elizabeth until the time of her delivery, when Elizabeth gets her second chance to speak. The helpful neighbors are there for the birth of Elizabeth's son and they are a part of the eighth-day naming of the child. In the way of busy helpers they have decided that the baby is to be named Zechariah after his father, who is still unable to speak. The naming of a child belongs to that parent, but Elizabeth speaks up: "No, he is to be called John."

This calls forth many objections because it is not a family name. The neighbors have no way of knowing that the angel told this name to Zechariah at the announcement of his conception. Coming from a root that means "God's gracious gift," it is a prediction of the child's place in history. At this moment it is a cause of confusion.

Someone makes a sign to the silent Zechariah who asks for a writing tablet on which he writes, "His name is John." That decides it. The father's tongue is loosed, Zechariah picks up his tiny son and he sings, in a voice that must have been a bit rusty, a song of blessing for God's goodness and a prediction of the prophetic life this child will lead.

Elizabeth must have been looking on with pride. She has played her part in bringing her baby into this world and she will presumably work with Zechariah to raise to manhood the one to be known as John the Baptist, he who will prepare the way for Jesus of Nazareth. She has nothing more to say. She recognized Mary's unborn child and she correctly named her son. It is enough.

~9~

WOMEN WHO SAID "LISTEN TO ME"

THE CAPTIVE SLAVE; ANNA THE WIDOW

There are moments in the Bible when a woman's voice is so clear that it must be heard.

~THE CAPTIVE SLAVE~

One of the most striking is found in 2 Kings 5. The Kingdom of Aram has been raiding in Israel and, as part of his booty, Naaman, commander of the army of Aram, has brought home an Israelite girl as a slave. That does not seem to be an auspicious beginning.

This Naaman, while a most skilled and trusted warrior, also suffers from leprosy. We need to remind ourselves that this is a generic biblical term for any skin disease. Whatever his affliction, it is seemingly incurable.

The slave, working with Naaman's wife, sighs with homesickness and tells her new mistress that if Naaman were in her homeland the great prophet at work there would surely cure him. The wife tells Naaman, who tells the king of Aram, and this latter is willing to do anything to find a cure for his right-hand man.

There was a long-standing belief that persisted through the Renaissance that monarchs had power to heal, so the king sends Naaman to the king of Israel with a large sum of money and the gift of ten sets of garments. This latter is upset when the gifts and the leprous general arrive at his home. He suspects some kind of plot and rends his garments in protest.

Elisha the prophet sends word to the king to have his unwelcome visitor come to his house so that he might see the power of God. Accordingly, the retinue of horses and chariots is redirected and draws up before Elisha's front door. The prophet does not appear. Instead he sends a message to Naaman to go and wash seven times in the Jordan River. This is not what Naaman expects.

He becomes infuriated and protests to his retinue that he thought the great man would come out and call on his God and wave his hand over the leprosy. In a rage he sputters, "Are not the rivers of Damascus better than all the waters of Israel?" He probably looked with less than admiration at the little Jordan flowing past him.

His servants are of a different mind. They calm him by noting that if the prophet had told him to do something difficult, would he not have done it? Why not dip into this river since they are here beside it? Naaman calms down enough to listen, and he follows Elisha's order with healing results. He returns to the prophet's house to present his gifts, but Elisha refuses. He healed no one. It was his God who did it.

Naaman then asks permission to take two mule loads of earth from Israel back to Aram. This comes from the belief that every land was ruled by its own god, whose power was limited to that land. If this God of Elisha had power over Israel, Naaman needed a bit of Israel in his homeland so that he could pray to him on his own soil. He wishes from now on to honor this God. Moreover, he says that from now on he will pray and offer sacrifice to none except the God of Israel. He humbly adds that the only exception will be when his master goes into the temple of Rimmon and needs to lean on his arm. Then he will ask God to pardon him as he renders this service. Elisha blesses Naaman and sends him off.

We are left to imagine his return to an ecstatic wife who helps as he spreads the earth of Israel in the garden for his prayer purposes. He is watched by a very satisfied little slave who knew her God was more powerful than any deity in this pagan land. She is generous enough to share faith in her God with the pagan who has captured her. While she remains nameless, her charming story belongs to all of us.

~ANNA THE WIDOW~

Knowing when to speak and when to wait is a gift. Nine centuries later there is a similarly wise woman in chapter 2 of Luke's gospel. She is too often overlooked and few authors underline this first apostle of the Good News. To meet her we need to step into the courtyard of the Temple in Jerusalem. Two elderly people are there. Everyone has seen them, seemingly forever. Who are they?

One is Simeon, a devout Jew who is convinced that he will not die until he has seen the Lord's Messiah. He haunts the courtyard, scanning the faces of those who come with their newborn sons, waiting for the One who will allow him to close his eyes in peace. But he is not alone. Beside him is Anna, a widow who is now eighty-four years old. As a widow she belongs to the poorest of the poor, those who have lost husbands and who have no sons and no male kinsmen to protect them. She too will have her moment.

She has been coming to the Temple daily, praying, waiting, longing. She and Simeon must have their little regular rituals, their daily greetings and exchanges of news, their times of prayer and of mutual encouragement. Since Anna is referred to as a "prophet" there must have been those who sought her counsel and her prayers. Day follows day and they wait until the morning when they are rewarded.

Mary and Joseph come into the courtyard with their child and their offering of the poor, two small birds. This is Simeon's moment. He takes the baby in his arms — the parents must have been startled — and begins to sing his song of gratitude that he has lived to see this day. In all the ordinary comings and go-ings in that bustling courtyard, the normal foot traffic did not halt. Only the parents heard his proclamation that the baby would one day be light for the Gentiles and glory for Israel.

Though given no recorded words, it is Anna's role to "speak about the child to all who were looking for the redemption of Jerusalem." (Luke 2:38) This makes her the first apostle of the New Testament. She has lived this long so that her voice, that of a poor widow, is the first to proclaim the Good News. It is a delightful moment near the end of her very long life and she uses it to the fullest.

Conclusion

We have met them, named and nameless. We have walked with them across desert sands and into palace courtyards. We have suffered with their losses, rejoiced at their courage, and found that beneath the clothing of past eras, the human heart is not different from ours.

We will not be called upon to make their decisions nor to suffer their consequences. We will have to make our own decisions in our own circumstances, and for this they can serve as models. They live in patriarchy because that is all their world knows. They find their way to shape their lives, some with success and some with a bleaker ending. We cannot ignore them.

Having read their stories, we have much to reflect on. It is astonishing that the male recorders of the Bible (almost certainly the human authors were male scribes) have given us these moments. The women as family storytellers undoubtedly helped to shape the ancestor accounts. Did they quietly but firmly make certain they were included?

It is intriguing to imagine a Hebrew mother gathering her children about her before bedtime to tell stories of the past and to make sure that Abraham's includes Sarah's as well, that Isaac's rather pallid adult life is enlivened by that of the creative Rebekah...

However it came about, the story of biblical women is ours to explore, even as we remind ourselves that to describe is not to prescribe. Such injustice has been done to the Bible, God's gift to us, by the narrow interpretation that everything it records is to be forever imitated. How things were is not how things should be in other generations. God trusted the human beings to whom he gave intelligence and free will to read their ancestor accounts using those same faculties.

We realize too that the Hebrew people grew theologically through the centuries recorded in the books of the Bible. The early ancestors did not yet have a belief in life beyond this one, so all had to be made right now. By the time of the New Testament, Jesus would dialogue with Pharisees who believed in a life to come and with Sadducees who did not. Where one stands on these issues affects how one lives.

Those of us in the Western world today see women in a dramatically different way from what is recorded in the Bible. We want them to be educated and capable of living an economically independent life, if that is what they choose. Our businesswoman is quite different from Martha of Bethany or Tamar of Canaan. Or is she?

There is a kinship that defies the externals

of time and place. It is that which we seek from a study of these intriguing women who invite us to see them where they lived and how they lived even as they say, "What might you have done had you been me?"

We owe them our gratitude and our admiration for opening to us other facets of the inexhaustible riches of this biblical library. We are richer for knowing them, and we delight in their being part of the great biblical story of God at work in our world. What more can we say but thank you?

Acknowledgments

No person ever writes a book alone. Some of my sources must be mentioned here:

A huge part of who I am and what I do is because I have been blessed to be part of a community of religious women, the Sisters of St. Ursula, with more than 400 years of history of working with and for women. This has been a pure gift.

I also must include all those who have asked me to speak at dinners and breakfasts, who have met some of these biblical woman during retreat times and then have urged me to write them down. Each and all of you deserve my gratitude.

Without the steady hand and clear voice of Bob Asahina, my editor and cheerleader, nothing would have come to pass. I thank him for his encouragement and stimulus, and, above all, for his saying, "Write that book." "Thank you" is insufficient, but here it is anyway.

Catherine Gormley, SU, fellow lover of the Word, you alone know the gift of our discussions over suppers and lunches, of your patiently reading the initial text and making helpful suggestions, and of your calm in assisting a computer novice. I am beyond grateful.

I also owe thanks to Califia Suntree, who copyedited the manuscript and who helped me through the throes of proofing it. I hope some day to express my appreciation in person.

A special mention must be made of the Marble Church community. You know, I hope, the role you have played in helping these biblical women find a foothold. You have questioned, showed up for class, brought me your conundrums, and urged me to put these women into print. There is no adequate word for my gratitude to so many of you.

The ministers and staff of Marble Church have helped me find new meaning in "the joy of work." You are the best!

Finally, I owe gratitude to Linda Phillips Ashour, whose friendship started everything that turned my life upside down and thrust me into the literary world. *Merci beaucoup*!

ABOUT THE AUTHOR

Carol M. Perry, SU, is the Resident Bible Scholar at Marble Collegiate Church in New York City. She is the author of *Waiting for Our Souls to Catch Up*, one of AARP's "Best Books of 2014," and the coauthor of *Called and Sent*. She has been a recipient of two National Endowment for the Humanities grants, was selected as an Educator of the Year by the Association of Teachers of New York, and has lectured across the country on scripture, Christian feminism, and the role of women in the Biblical world. A Sister of St. Ursula, she is a graduate of Fordham University and earned an MA in theology at St. Mary's, Notre Dame.

Sister Carol's blog can be found here: www.marblechurch.org/connect/blogs/sister-carol-perry